Editor
Wanda Kelly

Managing Editor
Ina Massler Levin, M.A.

Editor-in-Chief
Sharon Coan, M.S. Ed.

Art Director
CJae Froshay

Art Coordinator
Denice Adorno

Cover Design
Lesley Palmer

Imaging
Rosa C. See

Production Manager
Phil Garcia

Publishers
Rachelle Cracchiolo, M.S. Ed.
Mary Dupuy Smith, M.S. Ed.

Blake Staff

Editor
Sharon Dalgleish

Designed and typeset by
The Modern Art Production
Group

Printed by
Australian Print Group

Grammar
PRACTICE

Grades 3–4

Author

Peter Clutterbuck

This edition published by
Teacher Created Materials, Inc.
6421 Industry Way
Westminster, CA 92683
www.teachercreated.com

©2002 Teacher Created Materials, Inc.
Reprinted, 2002

Made in U.S.A.

ISBN-0-7439-3621-3
with permission by
Blake Education
Locked Bag 2022
Glebe NSW 2037

Contents

Contents *(cont.)*

Introduction

This second book of *Grammar Practice* for third and fourth grades provides teachers with resources, activities, and ideas aimed at introducing students to the basic elements of grammar. The activity pages can be used as a resource around which to build and develop a classroom program.

Good grammar skills help children improve their expression and give them an appreciation of how the various elements of English are used to convey meaning. With an understanding of the rules, processes, and elements that govern English, children are able to communicate both correctly and effectively.

In the past, lessons in grammar often became irrelevant and meaningless to students because of the tendency to stress the elements rather than focus on the functions of the elements. *Grammar Practice* ensures that the functions of elements such as parts of speech, phrases, and sentences are related to expression in a practical and purposeful way.

Grammar Practice is designed to make it as easy as possible to find what you need. Photocopiable work sheets are grouped according to grammatical element, and each of these elements is introduced with a definition and examples for the teacher, followed by a collection of appropriate and motivating teaching strategies. With the three books in *Grammar Practice*, teachers can create an individual and comprehensive grammar program for their students.

How to Use This Book

The *Grammar Practice* series aims to improve children's ability to

• use language effectively in their own writing,

• use language accurately in their own writing,

• read critically the writing of others.

With this in mind, the books have been designed to make it easy for teachers to find the following:

The grammatical elements to teach at each level
• Refer to the overview provided by the assessment checklist.
• Read the background information to find the terminology and depth of treatment appropriate.

Concise background information about each grammatical element
• This is located in the introduction to each grammatical element.

Practical strategies showing how to teach each grammatical element
• Use motivating activities as starting points to introduce a grammatical element and capture children's interest.
• Use other proven strategies to explicitly teach or model a grammatical element.
• Use games for reinforcement.

Blackline master (BLM) work sheets to reinforce learning
• They are a comprehensive resource around which to build a program.

Systematic teaching
Children need a solid general framework of grammatical understanding and skills to support their learning across the curriculum. To provide this framework, you may want to teach certain grammatical elements in a systematic way. The assessment checklists provided in each level of *Grammar Practice* indicate the grammatical elements that students should understand by the end of each level. The checklists can be used to program your systematic teaching and to record children's achievements.

Incidental teaching
Incidental teaching is an important strategy to use to help students build on prior learning and develop their understanding of grammar in context. A grammar lesson might, therefore, stem from the context of different texts students are reading and writing or from the need to deal with a specific problem individual children or groups of children are experiencing in their own writing. To teach at this point of need, simply dip into *Grammar Practice* and find the appropriate information, strategies, or work sheets for your children.

Assessment

To be successful, any grammar program must be accompanied by regular assessment. The methods used may differ from teacher to teacher but should encompass basic points.

For each student, assessment should accomplish the following:

(a) record clearly the progress being made;

(b) indicate the future steps being planned for reinforcement and extension;

(c) indicate specific areas of difficulty and possible remediation;

(d) use various strategies to determine whether an outcome has been achieved;

(e) be a relevant and careful measurement of the stage of grammar development;

(f) provide clear and precise suggestions to parents as to how they may best assist at home;

(g) provide clear and precise information to teachers.

Assessment Checklist

Name _____   Quarter

Parts of Speech	1	2	3	4
Identifies and uses correctly				
different types of nouns				
action, saying, and thinking verbs				
simple past, present, and future tenses				
subject-verb agreement				
a variety of adjectives				
a variety of adverbs				
degrees of comparison				
definite and indefinite articles				
prepositions as position words				
personal and possessive pronouns				
conjunctions to link ideas				
Vocabulary				
Identifies				
base words				
suffixes and prefixes				
similes				
Sentences				
Identifies and writes				
sentences that make sense				
question, statement, exclamation, command				
direct and indirect speech				
descriptive phrases				
sentences with more than one clause				
Punctuation				
Uses				
capital letters, periods				
question marks, exclamation marks				
commas				
apostrophes for contractions				
Experiments with				
colon, semicolon, dash				
quotation marks				

Comments

Areas of strength
_____

Areas of difficulty
_____

Steps being undertaken to reinforce areas of difficulty or extend grammar skills
_____

Parts of Speech

Every name is called a **noun**,
As *fence* and *flower*, *street* and *town*;

In place of noun the **pronoun** stands,
As *he* and *she* can raise their hands;

The **adjective** describes a thing,
As *magic* wand and *twisted* string;

The **verb** means action, something done—
To *read* and *write*, to *jump* and *run*;

How things are done the **adverbs** tell,
As *quickly*, *slowly*, *badly*, *well*;

The **preposition** shows the place,
As *in* the street or *at* the base;

Conjuntions join, in many ways,
Sentences, words, *or* phrase *and* phrase.

anonymous

Nouns

Introduction

Third and fourth grade students should be made familiar with the following functions of a **noun**.

(a) Nouns are the **names** of things around us. Nouns that are used to name general things (rather than a particular person or thing) are called **common nouns**.

Examples: *dog* *table* *car* *bottle*

(b) Some nouns are the names of particular or special people or things. These are called **proper nouns** and are written with a capital letter at the beginning.

Examples: *Katy* *Ben* *October* *North Carolina*
United States *Christopher Columbus*

(c) Some nouns are the names we use for collections of things. These are called **collective nouns**.

Examples: *flock* of birds *herd* of cattle *bunch* of grapes

Other collective nouns name a number of different things in the same class.

Examples: *fruit* *fish* *luggage* *team*

(d) Nouns can be singular or plural. The relevant plural constructions at this level are the following:

• Many plurals are made by simply adding *-s*.
Examples: *dog/dogs* *girl/girls*

• If the noun ends in *-s, -sh, -ch,* or *-x*, make the plural by adding *-es*.
Examples: *bus/buses* *bush/bushes* *church/churches* *fox/foxes*

• If the noun ends in a *-y* before which there is a consonant, make the plural by changing *-y* to *-i* and adding *-es*.
Examples: *fairy/fairies* *city/cities*

• If the noun ends in *-y* before which there is a vowel (*a, e, i, o, u*), make the plural by simply adding *-s*.
Examples: *monkey/monkeys* *toy/toys*

• If the noun ends in *-f*, change the *-f* to *-v* and add *-es*.
Examples: *loaf/loaves* *leaf/leaves*

However, some simply add *-s*.
Examples: *roof/roofs* *chief/chiefs*

Nouns *(cont.)*

- Some nouns have an irregular plural.

   Examples: *foot/feet   goose/geese   man/men   child/children*

(e) **Possessive nouns** are especially difficult for children at this level to grasp.

- The possessive of a singular noun is formed by adding an apostrophe and *-s* at the end of the word. No letters are changed or left off the original word.

   Examples: the *boy's* dog (The boy owns a dog.)
   the *lady's* car (The lady owns a car.)

- The possessive of a plural noun ending in *-s* is formed by adding an apostrophe.

   Examples: horses/*horses'* manes   ladies/*ladies'* cars

- The possessive of a plural noun not ending in *-s* is formed by adding an apostrophe and *-s*.

   Examples: children/*children's*   men/*men's*

(f) **Terms of address** are the nouns we use when we refer to or address certain people.

   Examples: *Mr.* Jones   *Ms.* Smith   *Doctor* Smith   *Captain* Peters

Children should also be introduced to the relationship of nouns to words such as verbs (words that tell what the noun is doing), adjectives (words that describe the noun), and pronouns (words that take the place of a noun).

Teaching Strategies

Mystery bag

Fill a cloth bag with a variety of small objects. Have children feel the outside of the bag to see if they can identify any objects.
They can write the names of the things they have identified on a sheet of paper.

Alphabet game 1

Challenge children to write a common noun for every letter of the alphabet. Make the challenge more exciting by adding a time limit.

Alphabet game 2

Challenge children to write a proper noun for every letter of the alphabet. Make the challenge more exciting by adding a time limit.

Nouns (cont.)

Listing time

Challenge children to write or say in a set time a set number of nouns in a certain category.

Name ten types of birds.   (sparrow, dove, emu ...)
Name ten children in this grade.   (Chan, Mike, Sally ...)

Collective class

Write a list of nouns on the chalkboard. Now give the collective noun to describe the class one of the words belongs to. Ask the children to identify the matching noun from the list.

diamond	apple	desk
snake	cricket	daisy

What noun is a reptile?   *What noun is a flower?*

I spy

Have children challenge each other to discover the name of a secret object somewhere in the classroom.
I spy with my little eye something that begins with the letter "c."
Children can take turns guessing until they arrive at the correct answer.

Magazine search

Have children search through old magazines and newspapers for the names of special things (proper nouns) in certain categories. They could try cities, countries, streets, and so on.

Cutouts

Have children cut out a large shape and inside write the names of things that belong to that group, for example, bird names inside a bird shape. The name shapes can then be displayed around the room.

Made-up collections

After discussing common collective nouns with children (a flock of birds, a herd of cattle), have them make up their own imaginary collective nouns that they feel would suit a group of creatures.

a slither of snakes   *a hop of frogs*
a gathering of iguanas   *a trumpet of elephants*

WORD BANK

Nouns

Common Nouns

arm	father	river
aunt	fish	road
baby	fox	school
bird	girl	sea
boat	house	ship
book	ice	sister
boy	lake	star
car	mother	street
coat	nest	tree
day	pet	window
dog	pie	year
ear	pond	zoo

Proper Nouns

Aunt Tanya
Christopher Columbus
Christmas
Christmas Day
Doctor Smith
Easter
Long Island
the White House
Empire State Building
World Trade Center
President Washington
Lake Placid
Mississippi River
Mount McKinley
Sesame Street

Collective Nouns

army
band
bunch
class
crew
family
flock
forest
gang
herd
litter
pack
swarm
team
troop

Common Nouns

Name _____ Grammar BLM **1**

Nouns that are used to name general things are called common nouns.

1. Which noun best completes each sentence?

flag   apple   puppy   rain   creek   coat   pie   atlas

a. A baby dog is called a _____ .

b. As it was so cold, I decided to wear a _____ .

c. The United States _____ has 50 stars on it.

d. I ate a meat _____ for lunch.

e. An _____ is a type of fruit.

f. A book of maps is called an _____ .

g. A small river is called a _____ .

h. Drops of water that fall from clouds are called _____ .

2. Choose the correct name and write it in the space.

a. We filled the _____ with water. (**battle, bottle**)

b. The present was wrapped in a sheet of pink _____ .
(**paper, pepper**)

c. A _____ can climb trees quickly. (**donkey, monkey**)

d. A _____ can be paddled across the lake. (**coat, boat**)

e. The _____ ate all the pieces of cheese. (**mouth, mouse**)

f. I bought some lollipops at the candy _____ . (**ship, shop**)

g. We get _____ from cows and goats. (**milk, silk**)

h. A part of a flower is called a _____ . (**petal, metal**)

Common Nouns

Nouns that are used to name general things are called common nouns.

1. Write the common noun.

kitten	peach	shirt	golf	swan	gold
canoe	lion	ant	piano	snail	kettle

a. a small boat _____

b. a fruit _____

c. a baby cat _____

d. a creature with a shell _____

e. a very large cat _____

f. a container for boiling water _____

g. something you wear _____

h. a musical instrument _____

i. a large water bird _____

j. an insect _____

k. a valuable metal _____

l. a sport _____

2. **All ten common nouns in the grid have only three letters. Find the nouns and write them on the lines.**

c	a	r	h	a	t
b	b	a	l	e	f
u	o	r	o	a	o
s	x	m	g	r	x
i	c	e	k	e	y

_____ _____

_____ _____

_____ _____

_____ _____

_____ _____

Common Nouns

Name _____   Grammar BLM **3**

Nouns that are used to name general things are called common nouns.

1. Use a common noun from the box to complete each line.

| ant | fire | sugar | feather | snail | ice | deer | bat |

a. as fast as a _____

b. as slow as a _____

c. as light as a _____

d. as busy as an _____

e. as blind as a _____

f. as cold as _____

g. as sweet as _____

h. as hot as _____

2. Color red the boxes that contain the names of parts of your body. Color blue the boxes that contain the names of parts of your home.

window	curtain	cupboard	hair
ear	eye	roof	bathroom
bedroom	teeth	toe	ankle
nose	carpet	shelf	floor
door	hand	elbow	neck

Common Nouns

Nouns that are used to name general things are called common nouns.

1. Sort the common nouns under the headings.

tree	honey	jam	ice cream	bread	ropes
wood	sand	cups	butter	cardboard	pies

Things we can eat

_____

_____

_____

_____

_____

Things we can't eat

_____

_____

_____

_____

_____

2. Sort the common nouns under the headings.

chair	elephant	table	cow
stool	magpie	boy	sparrow
lion	lady	ladder	penguin

Things with four legs

_____

_____

_____

_____

Things with two legs

_____

_____

_____

_____

Proper Nouns

Name _____   Grammar BLM **5**

Proper nouns are the names of particular people, places, or things. They begin with capital letters.

1. Add a word from the box to complete each sentence.

| days | students | months | planets | cities | countries |

   a. England, Vietnam, and China are all _____.

   b. Monday, Sunday, and Friday are all _____ of the week.

   c. Katy, Mat, and Ian are all _____ at my school.

   d. July, August, and September are all _____ of the year.

   e. Chicago, Dallas, and Miami are all_____ .

   f. Mars, Jupiter, and Venus are all _____ in our solar system.

2. Use the proper nouns in the box to complete the story.

| Rover | July | Tuesday | Michael | Christmas |
| Disneyland | | Joanna | | California |

"Next _____, which is the 15th of _____, is my birthday," said

_____. "My parents are going to take me to _____ in

_____as a treat. My sister, _____ , is also coming,

but I am going to leave my dog,_____ , at home. I might take him with

me when I go camping next _____ ."

Proper Nouns

Proper nouns are the names of particular people, places, or things. They begin with capital letters.

1. **Write an answer for each question.**

   a. What is your favorite day of the week? _____

   b. What is your favorite month of the year? _____

   c. What country would you like to visit? _____

   d. What is the name of your teacher? _____

   e. What is the name of your school? _____

   f. What are the names of three other students in your class?

   _____

2. **Address the envelope to yourself. Don't forget to start each proper noun with a capital letter. You may design your own postage stamp.**

Collective Nouns

Name _____   Grammar BLM **7**

Collective nouns are the names we use for collections of things.

1. Choose a collective noun from the box to write on each line.

> bunch   flock   herd   forest   swarm

   a. a _____ of cattle

   b. a _____ of grapes

   c. a _____ of bees

   d. a _____ of trees

   e. a _____ of birds

2. Use the words in the box to complete the story.

> album   string   deck   brood   bundle   box

In the old box Sally found a _____ of pearls, a _____ of matches, and an old _____ of playing cards. Suddenly, as she lifted a _____ of rags, she saw an _____ of stamps. She grabbed the stamps and raced outside to show her father who was feeding the _____ of chickens that had just hatched.

3. Write the word from the box that names each group or class of things.

> fruit   birds   furniture   insects

   a. hawks, eagles, and doves   _____

   b. ants, bees, and grasshoppers   _____

   c. apples, pears, and bananas   _____

   d. tables, chairs, and benches   _____

Collective Nouns

Name _____   Grammar BLM **8**

Collective nouns are the names we use for collections of things.

1. Write each noun under its collective heading.

| banana | chair | stool | zebra | table | swan | dove | lion |
| giraffe | horse | eagle | apple | peach | desk | emu | pear |

Animals   Birds   Fruit   Furniture

_____   _____   _____   _____

_____   _____   _____   _____

_____   _____   _____   _____

_____   _____   _____   _____

2. Write the word from the box that names each group or class of things.

| people | countries | meat | vegetables | flowers | fruit |

a. uncle, aunt, boy, and girl   _____

b. daisy, rose, daffodil, and pansy   _____

c. lettuce, turnip, potato, and bean   _____

d. chop, sausage, steak, and lamb   _____

e. lemon, orange, lime, and apricot   _____

f. Australia, China, Vietnam, and Spain   _____

3. Match each collective noun to the group it names.

| cards | people | grapes | beads | students | players |

a. a class of _____   **d.** a deck of _____

b. a team of _____   **e.** a crowd of _____

c. a bunch of _____   **f.** a string of _____

Plural Nouns

Singular nouns refer to one person, place, or thing.
Plural nouns refer to more than one person, place, or thing.

1. Write the correct word on the line.

a. Mr. Smith has two _____ on his arm. (watch, watches)

b. Freya has three blue _____. (dress, dresses)

c. The gardener cut down all the _____. (tree, trees)

d. The fairy gave me three _____. (wish, wishes)

e. My mother took all the _____. (brush, brushes)

f. There are a lot of _____ at our school. (class, classes)

2. Circle the plural nouns. Hint: There might be more than one in a sentence.

a. The men swept the leaves.

b. The cats climbed the fence.

c. The birds flew into the trees.

d. The horses ate some grass.

e. The donkeys kicked the gate.

f. The buses stopped at all the schools.

3. Write the plural nouns.

a. one child, two _____

b. one ball, four _____

c. one boat, two _____

d. one mouse, four _____

e. one monkey, two _____

f. one man, four _____

Plural Nouns

Name _____   Grammar BLM **10**

Singular nouns refer to one person, place, or thing.
Plural nouns refer to more than one person, place, or thing.

1. Write the plural nouns on the lines.

a. one toy, two _____

b. one city, two _____

c. one lady, two _____

d. one puppy, two _____

e. one cart, two _____

f. one party, two _____

2. Complete each sentence by writing the singular of the noun in parentheses.

a. I killed the _____ that landed on the cake. **(flies)**

b. I saw a _____ in the pasture. **(donkeys)**

c. Ian ate the _____ for lunch. **(jellies)**

d. The ice cream had a _____ on top. **(cherries)**

e. The _____ looks clear today. **(skies)**

f. I saw a laser _____ hit his body. **(rays)**

3. Complete each sentence by writing the plural of the noun in parentheses.

a. There were three _____ in the forest. **(wolf)**

b. The waiter put all the _____ on the table. **(knife)**

c. The police caught the three _____. **(thief)**

d. Put the books on the _____. **(shelf)**

e. We cut the oranges into _____. **(half)**

f. It is said that a cat has nine _____. **(life)**

Possessive Nouns

Name _____ Grammar BLM **11**

An apostrophe is used to show possession (that something belongs to something or someone). The possessive of a singular noun is formed by adding an *apostrophe* and *-s* at the end of the word.

1. **Rewrite each phrase, using the possessive form of the noun. The first one has been done for you.**

   a. the ears of the dog _____ the dog's ears _____

   b. the claws of the cat _____

   c. the rattle of the baby _____

   d. the car of the teacher _____

   e. the beak of the bird _____

2. **Write an apostrophe where it is needed.**

   a. My sisters toys are in the box.

   b. Katys mother will bring the pencils.

   c. The womans papers blew away.

   d. My fathers shoes are too big for me.

   e. The mans suitcases were heavy.

3. **Write a sentence using the singular possessive of each noun.**

   a. horse _____

   b. cow _____

   c. lady _____

   d. car _____

Possessive Nouns

An apostrophe is used to show possession (that something belongs to something or someone). The possessive of a plural noun is formed by
- **adding an *apostrophe* if the word ends in *-s* (horses' manes)**
- **adding an *apostrophe -s* if the word does not end in *-s* (children's toys).**

1. Rewrite each phrase, using the possessive form of the noun. The first one has been done for you.

   a. the ears of the dogs _____ the dogs' ears _____

   b. the toys of the babies _____

   c. the food of the dogs _____

   d. the engines of the cars _____

   e. the hats of the children _____

2. Write an apostrophe where it is needed.

   a. The childrens lunches are in the basket.

   b. The horses tails were flicking.

   c. The birds nests are empty.

   d. The clowns noses were red.

   e. The mens suitcases are heavy.

3. Write a sentence using the plural possessive of each noun.

   a. cats _____

   b. cows _____

   c. women _____

   d. students _____

Terms of Address

Name _____   Grammar BLM **13**

Terms of address are the nouns used to refer to or address certain people. They begin with a capital letter and are often abbreviated (shortened) when they are used with proper names. However, when these words/nouns are not used with proper names, they are lowercase.

1. **Draw a line to match each term of address to its abbreviation.**

a.	doctor	mgr.
b.	manager	capt.
c.	colonel	maj.
d.	detective	lt.
e.	lieutenant	prof.
f.	captain	col.
g.	sergeant	p.m.
h.	major	sgt.
i.	prime minister	dr.
j.	professor	det.

2. **Use an abbreviation from the box to complete each sentence.**

Dr.	Mr.	Capt.	Ms.	Prof.	Det.

a. _____ Smith, the pilot of our airplane, told us we would arrive soon.

b. _____ Murphy has written a book which is a bestseller.

c. _____ Smith took my temperature.

d. Our next door neighbor, _____ Jones, rides her bicycle to work.

e. _____ Costa soon solved the crimes.

f. Our teacher, _____ Smith, likes us to work hard in class.

Nouns-Review

Name _____   Grammar BLM **14**

1. **Read the story and then write the proper nouns for the following:**

   a. the name of a town _____

   b. the name of a girl _____

   c. the name of a man _____

   d. the name of a cat _____

   e. the name of a month _____

   f. the name of a state _____

   g. the name of a woman _____

   h. the name of a day of the week _____

   i. the name of a city _____

Last Tuesday, which was the third of November, Simone and her brother, Jarrod, left their home in the city of Springfield. They traveled by train to a small town in Indiana called Richmond. When they arrived they were met by their grandparents, John and Mary Jones, who live on a farm beside Spoon River. After lunch Simone and Jarrod helped their grandfather put some bales of hay into the back of the new pickup. Rover, the dog, hopped on top of the hay. Cuddles, the cat, tried to come too but ran away when Rover barked.

2. **Find twelve words used as common nouns in the story above. Write them on the lines.**

_____   _____

_____   _____

_____   _____

_____   _____

_____   _____

Nouns-Review

Name _____

1. Write a collective noun in each space.

a. a _____ of cattle

b. a _____ of matches

c. a _____ of cards

d. a _____ of students

e. a _____ of birds

f. a _____ of bees

2. Rewrite the story, writing the underlined words in the plural.

The <u>lion</u> sat under the <u>tree</u> because it was so hot. The <u>fly</u> buzzed around, and the <u>lion</u> flicked <u>it</u> with <u>its</u> <u>tail</u>. On the <u>branch</u> of the <u>tree</u>, the <u>monkey</u> <u>was</u> nearly asleep. The <u>lion</u> growled loudly and shook <u>its</u> <u>mane</u>.

_____

_____

_____

_____

_____

_____

_____

3. Write the singular nouns.

a. two jellies, one _____

b. two buses, one _____

c. two ladies, one _____

d. two cities, one _____

e. two leaves, one _____

f. two halves, one _____

Verbs

Introduction

Third and fourth grade students need to develop an understanding of the following types of **verbs** and their uses.

(a) **Action verbs** are words that express a concrete action. They are common in spoken language and in the writing of young children.

Examples: *work   run   sit   eat   jump*

(b) **Saying verbs** express a spoken action.

Examples: *talk   tell   said   suggested   yelled*

(c) Some verbs do not express a concrete action—they express actions that happen mentally, such as feelings, ideas, thoughts, or attitudes. These can be called **thinking and feeling verbs**. They are common in arguments, narratives, and descriptions (but not scientific descriptions, which are objective).

Examples: I *like* Sam.   I *understand*.   Katy *believed* the story.
I *see* the rabbit.   I *think* people should recycle.

(d) Some verbs tell us about what things are and what they have. These are **being and having verbs**. They are common in all kinds of descriptions.

Examples: Ben *is* a good swimmer.
Ali *has* the answer.
They *are* here.

(*Is, are, has,* and *have* can also act as auxiliaries (or helping verbs) for doing, thinking, and feeling verbs. Example: Ben *is swimming*.)

Verbs have tenses. The tenses tell time and also can indicate continuation or completion. The three basic forms for every verb are the **present tense**, **past tense**, and **past participle**.

(a) **Present tense** indicates a certain action is going on now or that a certain state of condition is occurring in the present time.

I *walk* a mile every day.   We *walk* a mile every day.
You *walk* with your friend.   You *walk* to the store.
He/she/it *walks* alone.   They *walk* everywhere.

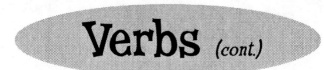
(b) Past tense indicates the action occurred yesterday or in some past time.

I walked a mile.	*We walked* a mile.
You walked with your friend.	*You walked* to the store.
He/she/it walked alone.	*They walked* everywhere.

(c) Past participle is a verb form that is used with *have, has,* or *had* to form the perfect tenses. It is always combined with an auxiliary (helper) to make a verb phrase. The following is the present perfect tense of the verb *to walk.*

I have walked a mile.	*We have walked* a mile.
You have walked with me.	*You have walked* daily.
He/she/it has walked alone.	*They have walked* home.

Children at this level should be able to talk about subject-verb agreement in a sentence. They are generally quick to identify times when the verb does not agree with the subject in number. If the subject is plural (more than one), a plural verb is required.

Examples: The *boys are* down the road.
The *girls like* ice cream.

If a subject is singular, a singular verb is required.

Examples: The *boy is* down the road.
The *girl likes* ice cream.

Teaching Strategies

Miming

Allow children to mime chosen activities and challenge classmates to guess what they are doing. Encourage classmates to answer in sentence form.

Tom is washing the dishes.

Freya is milking a cow.

Add a verb

Write a subject on the board and ask for volunteers to add suitable verbs.

Frogs _____ and _____ . (croak   hop)

Dogs _____ and _____ . (growl   bite)

Verbs *(cont.)*

Verb match

Prepare two sets of cards—one set with the names of a particular class of things (e.g., animals) written on them and one set with verbs to match written on them. Jumble the cards and challenge children to sort and match them.

cats	*fly*
dogs	*purr*
birds	*bark*

Puzzle verbs

On the chalkboard write the first letter of a verb and then a dash for each remaining letter. Tell the class what the verb means. Have volunteers add the missing letters.

g _ _ _ _ _   *to run like a horse*
w _ _ _   *to cry*

WORD BANK   Verbs

are	jump	see
call	like	shout
dive	mumble	sing
drink	play	smile
drive	push	stare
eat	read	swing
found	ride	tell
gather	roll	think
glide	run	throw
has	rush	walk
help	said	work
is	sang	yell

Verbs

Name _____

Action verbs express actions we can see, for example, *work, run, sit.*

1. Add an action verb to complete each sentence.

a. Sally _____ the ball I threw her.

b. Shunak _____ the button on the computer.

c. The horse _____ across the paddock.

d. Sumedha _____ a letter to her friend in India.

e. The savage dog _____ the stranger on the leg.

f. You may _____ when the bell rings.

2. Sort the action verbs under the headings below.

correct	dribble	rake
dig	run	read
water	kick	write

On the soccer field   At school   In the garden

_____   _____   _____

_____   _____   _____

_____   _____   _____

Verbs

Name _____ Grammar BLM **17**

Action verbs express actions we can see, for example, *work*, *run*, *sit*.

1. **Unjumble the letters in parentheses and write the action verb in the space.**

   a. Zach _____ the dishes. (**adwshe**)

   b. Please don't _____ the flowers. (**ipck**)

   c. Did you _____ your bicycle to school? (**irde**)

   d. The children will _____ from their friends. (**ihde**)

   e. He puts the sugar in the tea and then _____ it. (**stsir**)

   f. Be careful the cat does not _____ you. (**atchscr**)

2. **Add an action verb and a noun to complete each sentence.**

Action Verbs	Nouns
rode	soap
rocked	tree
ate	path
washed	cradle

   a. The giraffe _____ the leaves on the tall _____.

   b. The mother gently _____ the baby in the _____.

   c. I _____ my dirty clothes with _____ and water.

   d. Freya _____ the horse along the dusty _____.

Verbs

Saying verbs express spoken actions, for example, *talk, tell, said*.

1. Add a saying verb to complete each sentence.

> tell   quacked   screamed   said   talk   yelled

a. The ducks _____ when the dog came near.

b. The boy _____ across the playground to his friend.

c. The teacher will _____ us a story.

d. Ian _____ that he did not do it.

e. I will _____ to you on the phone tonight.

f. The children _____ when they saw the scary monster mask.

2. Write a sentence using each saying verb.

a. shouted _____

_____

b. whispered _____

_____

c. barked _____

_____

d. hooted _____

_____

e. hissed _____

_____

Verbs

Thinking verbs express actions that happen mentally, such as feelings, ideas, thoughts, or attitudes, for example, *I think people should recycle.*

1. Add a thinking verb to complete each sentence.

> felt   believed   understand   embarrassed   like   think

a. Do you_____ you can run faster than Ian?

b. I _____chocolate.

c. I _____happy on my birthday.

d. I _____the story.

e. I _____three different languages.

f. I _____my friend when I tripped.

2. Write a sentence using each thinking verb.

a. know _____

_____

b. dreams _____

_____

c. worried _____

_____

d. wanted _____

_____

Verbs

Name _____   Grammar BLM **20**

Action verbs express actions we can see, for example, *work, run, sit.*
Saying verbs express spoken actions, for example, *talk, tell, said.*
Thinking verbs express actions that happen mentally, such as feelings, ideas, thoughts, or attitudes, for example, I *like* Sam.

Circle the verb in each sentence. On the lines, write whether they are action, saying, or thinking verbs.

a. My dog loves sticks.   _____

b. Race me to the shop.   _____

c. He whispered the secret.   _____

d. I cheered for my team.   _____

e. I wish for more holidays.   _____

f. My dog barks at cars.   _____

g. I believe in Santa Claus.   _____

h. I told my teacher the truth.   _____

i. The horse galloped across the pasture.   _____

j. I dreamed about snakes last night.   _____

k. She shared her snack.   _____

Verb Tense

Name _____   Grammar BLM **21**

Verbs can tell us when an action is taking place.
If the action is happening now, it is called present tense.
I play football.
If the action has already happened, it is called past tense.
I played football yesterday.
If the action has not yet happened, it is called future tense.
I will play football tomorrow.

1. **These sentences are written in the present tense. Rewrite them in the past tense. The first one has been done for you.**

   a. I am a skater.
      I was a skater. _____

   b. Freya and Katy play soccer.

      _____

   c. Mike wants a pizza.

      _____

   d. Mr. Smith is a popular teacher.

      _____

   e. A black cat is good luck.

      _____

   f. I practice the piano.

      _____

2. **On the line, write whether the underlined verb is in the present, past, or future tense.**

   a. I <u>played</u> football yesterday.   _____

   b. We <u>will arrive</u> soon.   _____

   c. They <u>are</u> the best players.   _____

   d. The teacher <u>is</u> absent.   _____

   e. We <u>stayed</u> a long time.   _____

   f. I <u>will be</u> on the team next year. _____

Verb Tense

Verbs can tell us when an action is taking place.
If the action is happening now, it is called present tense.
I play football.
If the action has already happened, it is called past tense.
I played football yesterday.
If the action has not yet happened, it is called future tense.
I will play football tomorrow.

1. **Complete each sentence by writing the past tense of the verb in brackets.**

   a. Matt _____ the school bell this morning. (**ring**)

   b. I _____ my bicycle to school. (**ride**)

   c. We _____ many interesting things in the city. (**see**)

   d. Ian _____ all the candy. (**eat**)

   e. I _____ a picture of a snake in my book. (**draw**)

   f. It _____ very cold. (**is**)

2. **Now rewrite the sentences from section 1 in the future tense.**

   a. _____

   b. _____

   c. _____

   d. _____

   e. _____

   f. _____

Verb Tense

Name _____ Grammar BLM

Verbs can tell us when an action is taking place.
If the action is happening now, it is called present tense.
I play football.
If the action has already happened, it is called past tense.
I played football yesterday.
If the action has not yet happened, it is called future tense.
I will play football tomorrow.

Circle all the verbs in the story. Rewrite the story in the past tense, underlining the verbs.

I sit down and eat my breakfast. I bite my tongue, and it hurts. I feel bored, so I go outside and walk along the street. In the distance I see a car. I think it is a Toyota. The car comes towards me at great speed. I jump out of the way just in time. I go back inside. I trip over my skateboard in the hallway and crash into the hall cupboard. I stand up and bang my head on the open cupboard door. It is not a good day. I go back to bed.

_____

_____

_____

_____

_____

_____

_____

_____

_____

Verb Subject

To find the subject of a verb, ask who or what did something or is doing something. The answer is the subject.
Tom kicked the ball. Who kicked? The answer is Tom, so Tom is the subject.

1. **Circle the subject of the underlined verb.**

   a. Mrs. West <u>was</u> the teacher.

   b. The dog <u>buried</u> the bone.

   c. Susan <u>broke</u> the glasses.

   d. The batter <u>hit</u> a double.

   e. I <u>watch</u> films on television.

   f. Brian's grandfather <u>helped</u> him with his homework.

2. **This time underline the verb yourself and then circle the subject.**

   a. On a clear day Zach sees the mountains.

   b. Into the pool dived all the swimmers.

   c. You need your breakfast.

   d. In the classroom we hear the band in the hall.

   e. On the way to school she lost her watch.

   f. Across the misty mountains raced the bike riders.

Verb Subject and Object

Name _____   Grammar BLM **25**

In some sentences, the verb has a subject and an object.
To find the subject, ask who or what before the verb.
To find the object, ask who or what after the verb.

Mike   *kicked*   *the ball.*
subject   *verb*   *object*

1. Circle the subject. Then add an object to complete each sentence. The first one has been done for you.

   a. The (horse) kicked _____ the stable door _____.

   b. Jan won _____.

   c. Tom saw _____.

   d. The monkey climbed _____.

   e. Two boys found _____.

   f. The cat scratched _____.

2. These sentences sound silly because in each the verb's subject has been confused with its object. Rewrite each sentence correctly. The first one has been done for you.

   a. The banana ate a monkey.

   <u>The monkey ate a banana.</u> _____

   b. A goal kicked the captain.

   _____

   c. The boy bit a snake.

   _____

   d. A ball game played some girls.

   _____

   e. The cow milked the farmer.

   _____

   f. A book read Tom.

   _____

Subject and Verb

Name _____   Grammar BLM **26**

If the subject of a verb is plural (more than one), the verb should also be plural.
The boys are down the road.
The girls like ice cream.
If the subject of a verb is singular (only one), the verb should also be singular.
The boy is down the road.
The girl likes ice cream.

1. **Choose the correct verb from the parentheses and write it on the line.**

   a. The boys _____ towards the house. (**run runs**)

   b. That girl _____ in the park. (**play   plays**)

   c. Every day the lady _____ across the river. (**swim swims**)

   d. The children in that class _____ books. (**like likes**)

   e. After tea, Grandpa _____ in his chair. (**sit sits**)

   f. The girls often _____ stories about monsters. (**write writes**)

2. **Circle the correct verb in each set of parentheses.**

This (**is are**) my dog, Rover. He (**is are**) a German shepherd. German shepherds

(**is are**) good watchdogs. They (**is are**) big and strong. Rover (**is are**) black, but

many German shepherds (**is are**) a brown color. My favorite pets (**is are**) dogs, and

I think a German shepherd (**is are**) the best dog of all.

Adjectives

Introduction

Adjectives are words that tell us more about nouns or pronouns by describing them, adding details, or refining their meanings. By using adjectives, we can add meaning and interest to sentences. Third and fourth grade students should also come to understand that a completely different picture can be produced by changing the adjectives in a sentence.

Examples: The *resentful* girl showed the *cranky* lady the way.

The *kind* girl showed the *old* lady the way.

The *savage* dog chased the *frightened* boy.

The *playful* dog chased the *laughing* boy.

Children should be encouraged to think about the adjectives they choose and to steer away from adjectives that have become meaningless through overuse, such as *nice* and *good*.

Examples: It was a *nice* day.   It was a *sunny* day.

That was a *good* story.   That was an *exciting* story.

An adjective can come before or after the noun or pronoun it is describing.

Examples: The *big, black* dog ran home.

The *dog* was *big* and *black*.

There are many types of adjectives. Third and fourth grade students need to develop an awareness of the following types of adjectives and their uses.

(a) **Describing adjectives** are the most common. They are used to describe, or tell us about the quality of, a noun or pronoun.

Examples: *new   old   beautiful   ugly   big   small*

(b) **Demonstrative adjectives** (sometimes called determiners) are used to point out which noun is being spoken of.

Examples: *That* toy belongs to Katy.

This toy belongs to me.

Those boxes were taken away.

These boxes were left behind.

Adjectives (cont.)

(c) **Possessive adjectives** are used to show possession.

    Examples: This is *my* pen.
               Here is *your* hat.

The possessive adjectives follow:

	Singular	**Plural**
First person	my	our
Second person	your	your
Third person	his, her, its	their

(d) **Limiting or number adjectives** indicate number or quantity.

    Examples: *two* horses   *ten* fingers
              the *first* person in the line   the *second* month

Adjectives can change their form to indicate **degrees of comparison**. The three degrees follow:

Positive Degree—This is the simple form of the adjective.

    Examples: a *sweet* apple   a *muddy* boy   a *beautiful* rose

Comparative Degree—This is used when we compare two people or things. We usually add *-er* to the adjective, but for longer words we sometimes put *more* in front of the adjective.

    Examples: a *sweeter* apple   a *muddier* boy   a *more beautiful* rose

Superlative Degree—This is the highest degree and is used when we compare more than two people or things. It is made by adding *-est* to the adjective or putting *most* in front of the adjective.

    Examples: the *sweetest* apple   the *muddiest* boy   the *most beautiful* rose

Things to remember:

- Some adjectives add *-er* or *-est* without any change to their spelling.
  Examples: *tall*   *taller*   *tallest*

- Adjectives that end in *-e* drop the *-e* when adding *-er* or *-est*.
  Examples: *large*   *larger*   *largest*

- If the adjective ends in *-y*, the *-y* is changed to *-i* before adding *-er* or *-est*.
  Examples: *heavy*   *heavier*   *heaviest*

- In some adjectives the last letter is doubled before adding *-er* or *-est*.
  Examples: *big*   *bigger*   *biggest*

Adjectives *(cont.)*

- Adjectives of three syllables (and even some of two syllables) have *more* before them for the comparative degree and *most* before them for the superlative degree.
  Examples: *honest   more honest   most honest*
- Some adjectives have only a simple form. For example, a thing can only be *dead*; it cannot be "more dead."
  Examples: *full   empty   straight   perfect   correct*

Teaching Strategies

Get the chalk
One of the best ways to introduce adjectives to children of this age group is to ask a child to get something for you. For example you might say, "Joanne, would you get the chalk for me, please?" When Joanne arrives with the chalk say, "No. That's not the chalk I want." Give two or more children the same request, and when they become nonplussed, lead them into a discussion on the function of adjectives. You might then say, "I wanted the *blue* chalk inside the *old* box."

Describe the picture
Display a large picture to the class. Have children orally describe the nouns that are featured in the picture.
a pretty dress   a red ball   a shady tree   a delicious ice-cream sundae

Stretch the joke
Write a story or a short joke on the board. Underline all the nouns. Have children rewrite the story or joke, adding adjectives to the nouns.
Two caterpillars were eating grass in a garden when a butterfly flew overhead.
Two large, fat caterpillars were eating delicious grass . . .

Mystery bag
Place an object in a bag. Let children feel the object and then describe it to you.
It is soft.   It is round.   It is small.   It is rubbery.

Noun lists
Write a list of nouns on the chalkboard. Ask children to supply suitable describing words.

tiger:	*savage*	*hungry*	*striped*
elephant:	*big*	*gray*	*wrinkled*

Adjectives  *(cont.)*

Comparing adjectives

Ask a child to come to the front of the room and then ask a shorter and a taller child to stand on each side. Ask questions such as these:

Who is the tallest of the three?
Who is the shortest of the three?
Is Mary taller than Peter?
Of Joanne and Peter, who is the taller?

WORD BANK   Adjectives

all	green	smooth
any	happy	soft
bad	hard	some
best	huge	strong
better	interesting	tall
brave	kind	that
dark	little	these
deep	long	thick
eight	no	third
empty	one	this
every	open	those
fast	raw	tiny
fat	red	twelve
first	ripe	two
five	savage	white
four	second	yellow

Adjectives

Name _____

Describing adjectives are used to describe a noun or pronoun.

1. Complete each sentence by adding the correct describing adjective from the box.

soft	strong	empty	raw	fast	open

a. I put water in the _____ bucket.

b. We went through the _____ door.

c. A cheetah is a very _____ runner.

d. A pillow made of feathers is _____ .

e. We have to cook the _____ meat.

f. An elephant is a _____ animal.

2. Complete each sentence by adding the correct describing adjective from the box.

brown	red	white	black	green	blue

a. The cow ate the _____ grass.

b. Coal is _____ .

c. I dived into the _____ water.

d. I ate the _____ apple.

e. She drank the _____ milk.

f. A chocolate bar is usually _____ .

Adjectives

Describing adjectives are used to describe a noun or pronoun.

1. Complete each sentence by adding the correct describing adjective from the box.

| tiny | huge | sharp | long | savage | hard |

   a. I cut the bread with a _____ knife.

   b. A mouse is a _____ animal.

   c. A giraffe has a _____ neck.

   d. A whale is a _____ animal.

   e. A tiger is a _____ animal.

   f. An old crab has a _____ shell.

2. Add a describing adjective of your own in each space.

Last week a _____ boy and his _____ friend

were walking along a _____ street. They looked at the top of a

_____ tree and saw a _____ bird sitting on

a _____ branch. The bird swooped down and landed on a

_____ fence where it had started to build a _____ nest.

Adjectives

Describing adjectives are used to describe a noun or pronoun.

1. **Draw a line to match each describing adjective with a noun.**

   Describing Adjectives   Nouns

   fast   door

   open   peach

   hard   water

   hot   rock

   deep   runner

   interesting   hair

   dark   fire

   ripe   book

2. **In each sentence, rearrange the jumbled letters to make a describing adjective.**

   a. Tom is very _____ for his age. (**llta**)

   b. This is a very_____ building. (**lod**)

   c. Here is a _____ shirt. (**eancl**)

   d. This is a piece of_____ wool. (**lbue**)

   e. Matt does _____ writing in his book. (**enat**)

   f. This is a very_____ river. (**edep**)

Adjectives

Describing adjectives are used to describe a noun or pronoun.

1. **Read the passage and circle all the describing adjectives (not limiting, possessive, numerical, or demonstrative adjectives or articles). Then answer the questions below.**

My best friend, Chan, has black hair and large, brown eyes. One day he was walking along a busy street, bouncing his rubber basketball, when he heard a strange noise coming from the top of a tall oak tree. He looked up, and on the highest branch, he saw a magpie with a broken wing being attacked by a hawk. The hawk was brown and had a strong beak.

   a. What are Chan's eyes like? _____

   b. How good a friend is Chan to the writer? _____

   c. What color is Chan's hair? _____

   d. What type of street was Chan walking along? _____

   e. What type of noise did Chan hear? _____

   f. What was wrong with the magpie's wing? _____

2. **Add an adjective of your own to describe each noun.**

   a. a _____ teacher

   b. a _____ meal

   c. a _____ kite

   d. a _____ fish

   e. a _____ flower

   f. a _____ game

Adjectives

Describing adjectives are used to describe a noun or pronoun.

1. Write a suitable describing adjective in each space.

a. A _____ girl lifted a _____ table.

b. A _____ dog chased a _____ boy.

c. The _____ cat followed the _____ mouse.

d. It was a _____ day when we went to the _____ forest.

e. A _____ bird laid three _____ eggs in the nest.

f. I put the _____ milk back in the _____ refrigerator.

2. Now write two descriptive adjectives to complete these sentences.

a. Teachers should be_____ and _____ .

b. The grass was _____ and _____ .

c. The flowers were _____ and _____.

d. My dog is _____ and _____ .

e. My best friend is _____ and _____.

f. Books should be _____and _____.

Adjectives

Limiting or number adjectives are used to show the number of things or the numerical order of things.

Example: *two* horses   *ten* fingers

the *first* person in the line   the *second* month

1. **Complete each sentence by adding the correct number adjective from the box.**

> five   eight   twelve   four   two

a. There are _____ months in the year.

b. You have _____ fingers on each hand.

c. An octopus has _____ tentacles.

d. A bicycle has _____ wheels.

e. Most cars have _____ wheels.

2. **Read the passage and circle all the number adjectives.**

Thirty children entered the swimming races. Two girls tied to win the first race. The new boy won the second race. I missed the second and third races because I was buying a drink. The fourth race was my favorite. They threw one hundred corks into the pool and teams had to race to get as many as they could. My team won. We gathered forty corks. By the tenth race I was exhausted and ready to come home.

Adjectives

Demonstrative adjectives are used to point out which noun is being spoken of.
That book belongs to Katy.
This book belongs to me.

1. **Choose a demonstrative adjective from the box to use in each space.**

this	that	these	those

a. _____ gloves are mine, but _____ gloves are yours.

b. _____ glass belongs to me, and _____ glass is yours.

c. _____ books are mine, and _____ books are yours.

d. _____ boxes were taken away, but _____ boxes were left behind.

Possessive adjectives are used to show ownership.
This is *my* pen.
Here is *your* hat.

2. **Choose a word from the box to use as a possessive adjective in each space.**

my	their	her	its	our	your

a. The cat licked _____ paws.

b. _____ friend is funny.

c. Is that _____ car in the garage?

d. _____ dress and earrings were very expensive.

e. It was _____ dog that bit _____ dog.

Adjectives

Adjectives can change their form to show degrees of comparison.

Positive Degree	Comparative Degree	Superlative Degree
sweet	sweeter	sweetest
muddy	muddier	muddiest
beautiful	more beautiful	most beautiful

1. Write the comparative degree of each adjective in parentheses.

a. Mike is _____ than Paul. (**strong**)

b. Today is _____ than yesterday. (**hot**)

c. This apple is _____ than the one you have. (**red**)

d. This table is _____ than that one. (**heavy**)

e. I think I am _____ than you. (**lucky**)

f. This pie is _____ than that one. (**delicious**)

2. Write the superlative degree of each adjective in parentheses.

a. This is the _____ day all year. (**hot**)

b. This is the _____ place to hide. (**safe**)

c. Tom is the _____ boy in the school. (**reliable**)

d. A Clydesdale is the _____ horse of all. (**big**)

e. Joe is the _____ person in the fourth grade. (**noisy**)

f. Ms. Smith is the _____ person I know. (**brave**)

Adjectives

Adjectives can change their form to show degrees of comparison.

Positive Degree	Comparative Degree	Superlative Degree
sweet	sweeter	sweetest
muddy	muddier	muddiest
beautiful	more beautiful	most beautiful

1. Complete the table.

Positive Degree	Comparative Degree	Superlative Degree
smooth		
		thinnest
	luckier	
wise		
	more delicate	
		greenest
good	better	

2. Complete each sentence by choosing the correct adjective degree from the brackets.

a. Ned is _____ than Freya. (**older oldest**)

b. A cat is a _____ pet than a dog. (**better best**)

c. This summer is the _____ one. (**hotter hottest**)

d. Today is _____ than it was yesterday. (**colder coldest**)

Adverbs

Introduction

An **adverb** is a word that adds meaning to (describes or limits) a verb, an adjective, or another adverb.

There are many types of adverbs. The three most important types for third and fourth graders to recognize are the following:

(a) **Adverbs of Place**—These are used to show where something happens.
Example: I told him to come *here*.

(b) **Adverbs of Time**—These are used to show when something happens.
Example: He played *yesterday*.

(c) **Adverbs of Manner**—These are used to show how something happens.
Example: The child cried *loudly*.

Like adjectives, adverbs can change their form to indicate **degrees of comparison**. The three degrees follow:

Positive Degree—This refers to one person or thing.
Example: Tom can play *hard*.

Comparative Degree—This compares two people or things.
Example: Tom can play *harder*.

Superlative Degree—This compares more than two people or things.
Example: Of the three children, Tom can play the *hardest*.

Remember the following:

• To some adverbs, add *-er* and *-est* to form the comparative and superlative.
Example: *hard   harder   hardest*

• Adverbs that end in *-ly* have *more* and *most* placed before them to form the comparative and superlative.
Example: *silently   more silently   most silently*

• Some adverbs are irregular and must be learned individually.
Example: *badly   worse   worst*

• Some adverbs look like adjectives. You can tell they are adverbs if they add meaning to verbs, adjectives, and other adverbs. If they add meaning to a noun, they are adjectives.

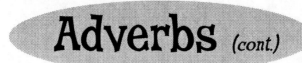
Adverbs (cont.)

Teaching Strategies

Give me one
Have children provide one adverb to replace a group of words in a sentence that is written on the chalkboard.
Mike always drives in a fast way.
Mike always drives quickly.

Adverb list
Have children list suitable adverbs to complete a sentence.
I can walk …
quickly   slowly   rapidly   proudly   lazily   awkwardly
Other suitable verbs to use for this exercise include swim, speak, creep, sleep, fight, wait, eat, laugh, dance, read, etc.

How game
Have sets of adverbs written on cards and distribute these to children. Now read out part of a sentence and have children hold up an appropriate card.

quickly   slowly   loudly   carefully

Synonyms and antonyms
Call out an adverb or write an adverb on the chalkboard. Have children provide an adverb of similar meaning or one of opposite meaning.

rapidly: quickly   slowly

WORD BANK   Adverbs

above	happily	seldom
already	helpfully	smoothly
behind	inside	sometimes
bravely	later	suddenly
cleverly	never	sweetly
early	now	then
everywhere	outside	today
gently	quietly	upstairs
greedily	roughly	well

Adverbs

An adverb is a word that adds meaning to a verb, an adjective, or another adverb. Adverbs of manner show how something happened. The cat hunted *quietly*.

1. **Choose an adverb of manner from the box to complete each sentence.**

   noisily   easily   slowly   greedily   silently   gently

   a. The starving dog ate the meat _____ .

   b. Mother put our baby to bed _____.

   c. The cat crept _____after the mouse.

   d. The fastest runner _____ won the race.

   e. The boy with the broken leg walked _____ down the street.

   f. When the teacher left, the class worked _____.

2. **Write sentences of your own that use these words as adverbs of manner.**

   a. softly _____

   _____

   b. quickly _____

   _____

   c. carefully _____

   _____

   d. sadly _____

   _____

   e. badly _____

   _____

   f. happily _____

   _____

Adverbs

Some adverbs look like adjectives. You can tell they are adverbs if they add meaning to verbs, adjectives, and other adverbs. If the words add meaning to a noun, they are adjectives.

1. Circle the adverb to complete each sentence.

    a. The girls played (happy happily) in the gymnasium.

    b. The teacher laughed (loud loudly) at my joke.

    c. David ran (quick quickly).

    d. I jumped the fence (easy easily).

    e. The teacher corrected our work (careful carefully).

    f. Jo held her trophy (proud proudly).

2. Change the word in parentheses into an adverb to complete each sentence.

    a. Ben can swim _____ . (**strong**)

    b. Ali cried _____ . (**sad**)

    c. The lady sang _____ . (**loud**)

    d. The mother sang _____ to her child. (**soft**)

    e. The teacher asked us to work _____ . (**neat**)

    f. The train came _____ into the station. (**slow**)

Adverbs

An adverb is a word that adds meaning to a verb, an adjective, or another adverb. Adverbs of place show where something happened.
I told him to come *here*.

1. **Use a place adverb from the box to complete each sentence.**

   out   here   there   somewhere   everywhere   near

   a. The supermarket is not far; in fact, it is quite _____ .

   b. The teacher said to put the extra book _____ .

   c. The terrible car accident occurred right _____ .

   d. Ian came in the back door as we went _____ .

   e. When the jar dropped, the candies scattered _____ .

   f. I was sure I put my brand new guitar _____ .

2. **Write sentences of your own that use these words as adverbs of place.**

   a. above _____

   _____

   b. downstairs _____

   _____

   c. in _____

   _____

   d. outside _____

   _____

   e. nowhere _____

   _____

   f. behind _____

   _____

Adverbs

An adverb is a word that adds meaning to a verb, an adjective, or another adverb. Adverbs of time show when something happened.
He played *yesterday*.

1. **Choose a time adverb from the box to replace the underlined words in each sentence.**

> later   now   yesterday   often   today   soon

a. Mike should arrive <u>in a short time</u>. _____

b. Don't wait for a moment; do it <u>right away</u>. _____

c. We went swimming <u>the day before today</u>. _____

d. We are going camping <u>this very day</u>. _____

e. There's no panic. You can finish it <u>in the future</u>. _____

f. Freya skips <u>lots of times</u>. _____

2. **Write sentences of your own that use these words as adverbs of time.**

a. seldom _____

_____

b. never _____

_____

c. then _____

_____

d. already _____

_____

e. before _____

_____

f. late _____

_____

Adverbs

An adverb is a word that adds meaning to a verb, an adjective, or another adverb.
- **Adverbs of manner show *how* something happened.**
- **Adverbs of place show *where* something happened.**
- **Adverbs of time show *when* something happened.**

1. **Look at the underlined adverb and write whether it tells how, when, or where.**

   a. I found it <u>there</u>. _____

   b. We crossed the busy road <u>carefully</u>. _____

   c. I asked her to come <u>here</u>. _____

   d. We should cut the lawn <u>today</u>. _____

   e. Are you playing football <u>tomorrow</u>? _____

   f. The child sat <u>sadly</u>. _____

2. **Choose the correct adverb to complete each sentence.**

   > here   now   there   soon   loudly   quickly

   a. The plants are growing _____ . (**how**)

   b. I will see you _____ . (**when**)

   c. Please come over _____ . (**where**)

   d. The angry dog barked _____ . (**how**)

   e. Put it down _____ . (**where**)

   f. I want you to do it right _____ . (**when**)

Adverbs

Adverbs can change their form to show degrees of comparison.

Positive Degree	Comparative Degree	Superlative Degree
hard	harder	hardest
softly	more softly	softest
well	better	best

1. **Fill the spaces with the correct adverb from the parentheses.**

   a. Bill jumps _____ than Tony. (**higher highest**)

   b. This apple tastes _____ than that one. (**better best**)

   c. The red car starts _____ than yours. (**easier easiest**)

   d. Take this pencil. It writes the _____ of all. (**better best**)

   e. Out of all the children, it was Meg who ran _____ . (**faster fastest**)

   f. A dog eats _____ than a cat. (**more most**)

   g. Sally played _____ than Peter. (**longer longest**)

   h. Of all the children, Tom sang the _____ . (**louder loudest**)

2. **Put the words in parentheses in their correct order in the sentences.**

   a. Mike did his work well. Sam did his work _____ . Zach did his work _____ of all. (**best better**)

   b. This red car travels _____ . Does the blue car go _____ ? Of the red, blue, and green cars, which travels the _____ ? (**faster fast fastest**)

Articles

Introduction

There are three **articles**: *the*, *a*, and *an*. Articles can be either definite or indefinite. Third and fourth grade students should be able to identify definite and indefinite articles. Articles function as adjectives in sentences.

(a) *The* is the **definite article**. It is definite because it is referring to a specific thing.
  Examples: *The* man lives next door.   *The* dog is outside.

(b) *A* and *an* are **indefinite articles**. Rather than referring to a specific thing, they refer to any one of a group of things.
  Examples: *A* man lives next door.   *A* dog is outside.

An is used instead of *a* in front of words that begin with a vowel (*a, e, i, o, u*). *An* is also used in front of words that begin with a silent *h*.

  Examples: *an* apple   *an* egg   *an* igloo   *an* orange
          an umbrella   *an* hour   *a* hotel   *an* homage

Teaching Strategies

I spy a vowel

Allow children to play I Spy in groups but limit their letter choices to the five vowels and possibly silent *h*. Playing games such as this will help those children still having difficulty identifying vowels—and thus help them to use *a* or *an* appropriately.

Noun detective

The articles can be used to determine whether or not a word is a noun. If a word makes sense or can be used in a sentence with an article before it, it can function as a noun. Because many words in our language can be used as more than one part of speech, the article noun test is a helpful tool. Have students apply the article noun test to words taken from their verb, adjective, adverb, and preposition lists.

Articles

The vowels of the alphabet are *a, e, i, o, u*.

1. **Circle the words in the box that contain all five vowels.**

> miscellaneous   education   cauliflower
> facetious   mountainous   mysterious

2. **Add the missing vowel or vowels to make the word. Write the word.**

a. s v n   (a number) _____

b. r n g   (a juicy fruit) _____

c. h r s   (an animal) _____

d. c r r t   (an orange vegetable) _____

e. n r   (close by) _____

f. c m l   (an animal) _____

3. **Make up some missing vowel puzzles of your own. Try them out on a friend.**

a. _____

b. _____

c. _____

Articles

The vowels of the alphabet are *a, e, i, o, u*. We use *an* instead of *a* in front of words that begin with a vowel.

1. **Write *a* or *an* in the spaces.**

   a. Would you like _____ egg for lunch?

   b. _____ zebra is black and white.

   c. _____ football player must train hard.

   d. What _____ easy thing to do!

   e. Have you seen _____ five-legged cow?

   f. Please let me have _____ turn.

   g. I ate _____ orange for my lunch.

   h. I read _____ book about dinosaurs.

2. **Write four nouns that begin with a vowel.**

   a. an _____

   b. an _____

   c. an _____

   d. an _____

3. **Write four adjectives that begin with a vowel.**

   a. an _____ dog

   b. an _____ baby

   c. an _____ toy

   d. an _____ car

Articles

When we are talking about a particular thing, we use *the*. This is called the definite article.

When we are talking about a general thing, we use *a* or *an*. This is called the indefinite article.

1. **Add *a*, *an*, or *the* in the spaces.**

   a. Ian can only do _____ underarm throw.

   b. I'd like to be _____ pilot when I grow up.

   c. Is this _____ ball you lost?

   d. John hit _____ winning run.

   e. The children said they had seen _____ elf in the garden.

   f. Is this _____ way to the swimming pool?

   g. _____ ink bottle is on the table.

   h. Megan is _____ best runner in our school.

2. **Complete the story by using *a*, *an*, or *the* in the spaces.**

There is _____ boy in my grade who is _____ best football player in _____

school. He is _____ very good swimmer too, but he is not _____ good citizen

because he has _____ bad temper. One day he threw _____ football through

_____ open door. It hit _____ boy who was sitting in _____ old chair near

_____ table that belongs to _____ teacher. _____ teacher was upset and

told _____ boy he would not be allowed to come on _____ field trip we

were having.

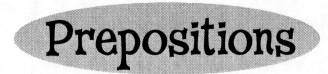

Introduction

Prepositions are words we use to show the relationship of a noun or a pronoun to another word in the sentence. They can be called place words because they often tell us the position of things.

> Example: The puppy is *on* the chair.
> The girl is *beside* the chair.
> The bone is *under* the chair.

The prepositions *on, beside,* and *under* all refer to the noun *chair*. They tell us the relationship between it and the puppy, the girl, and the bone. Also, each preposition has an object which is a noun or pronoun.

> Example: He sat on the *chair.*

Problem prepositions

among/between

Something is shared *among* several people (three or more). Something is shared *between* two people.

> Example: *I divided the cake among the whole class.*
> *I divided the cake between Mary and me.*

in/into

In shows position in one place. *Into* shows movement from one place to another.

> Example: *The teacher is in the room.*
> *The boy dived into the river.*

different from

One thing or person is *different from* another. Never say "different than."

beside/besides

Beside means at the side of. *Besides* means in addition to.

> Example: *The teacher stood beside the table.*
> *Several girls were there besides Margaret.*

Preposition or adverb?

Some prepositions may look like adverbs. To tell whether the word is a preposition or an adverb, look at the way it is used. Look at the following sentences.

> *I fell down. Down* is an adverb of place. It tells where I fell.

> *I walked down the road. Down* is a preposition governing *road*.

Remember also that a preposition always has an object (a noun or pronoun) after it.

Prepositions (cont.)

Teaching Strategies

Where is it?
Display a large picture. Have students explain the positions of certain objects in the picture.

Where is the canary?   *The canary is in the cage.*

Instruction games
Have children give a friend a series of instructions. The friend must carry out the instructions.

Go to the door. Then put your cap on the table and your backpack under the table.

Question time
Ask children to describe the positions of some objects in the classroom. Tell children they must reply by using a preposition in a sentence.

Where is the clock?   *The clock is under the picture.*
Where is the television?   *The television is beside the table.*

Preposition opposites
Have children provide the opposites of given prepositions.

The snake crawled <u>over</u> the rock.
The snake crawled <u>under</u> the rock.

WORD BANK   Prepositions

about	beyond	opposite
after	by	outside
against	during	over
along	except	since
around	for	through
at	from	to
before	in	under
behind	inside	underneath
below	into	until
beneath	near	up
beside	of	with
between	off	without

Prepositions

Prepositions show the relationship of a noun or a pronoun to another word in the sentence. The noun or pronoun follows the preposition.

1. Use a preposition from the box to complete each sentence.

through   during   in   over   up   under

a. There were six eggs _____ the magpie's nest.

b. A lot of homes were damaged _____ the storm.

c. The kangaroo jumped _____ the fence.

d. The children walked _____ the forest.

e. The little kitten was _____ the table.

f. She was the first person to climb all the way _____ the mountain.

2. Circle the correct preposition in parentheses.

a. Did they growl (**for   at**) you for breaking the window?

b. The teacher was angry (**with   to**) me.

c. The pear fell (**off   about**) the tree.

d. The bottle is full (**of   with**) water.

e. Let's sit here and wait (**after   for**) Ian.

f. Karen fell (**off   into**) the pool.

Prepositions

Prepositions show the relationship of a noun or a pronoun to another word in the sentence. The noun or pronoun follows the preposition.

1. **Add a preposition of your own to complete each sentence.**

   a. Matt ran all the way _____ the shop.

   b. The dog sleeps _____ a kennel.

   c. The frightened kitten hid _____ the table.

   d. I saw him running _____ the street.

   e. She leaned the shovel _____ the wall.

   f. The cat climbed quickly _____ the tree.

2. **Make sentences by combining the groups of words in the boxes. If you need more space, use the back of the sheet.**

The horses are	above	the kennel.
The boys are playing	in	the house.
The dog is sleeping	inside	the park.
The bird is flying	beside	the field.
The girls are picnicking	near	the stables.

_____

_____

_____

_____

_____

Prepositions

Prepositions show the relationship of a noun or a pronoun to another word in the sentence. The noun or pronoun follows the preposition.

1. Use the opposite preposition to fill each space.

over   above   after   around   off   outside

a. The dog crawled <u>under</u> the bush.

   The dog crawled _____ the bush.

b. We went <u>inside</u> the classroom.

   We went _____ the classroom.

c. We left <u>before</u> the bell rang.

   We left _____ the bell rang.

d. I looked at the hole <u>below</u> me.

   I looked at the stars _____ me.

e. The children sat <u>on</u> the branch.

   The children fell _____ the branch.

f. We rowed <u>across</u> the lake.

   We rowed _____ the lake.

2. Use a different preposition to complete each sentence.

a. Walk _____ the door.

b. Jump _____ the seat.

c. Look _____ the book.

d. Sit _____ your sister.

e. Run _____ the lawn.

f. Come _____ me.

Prepositions

Prepositions show the relationship of a noun or a pronoun to another word in the sentence. The noun or pronoun follows the preposition.

1. **Use a different preposition to complete each sentence.**

   a. A bird is sitting _____ the nest.

   b. The roots of a tree are _____ the branches.

   c. The snake is crawling _____ its hole.

   d. A cat is sleeping _____ the table.

   e. Ellen goes _____ her grandma's every weekend.

   f. A kangaroo is hopping _____ the fence.

2. **Read the story. Circle the prepositions.**

The children swam across the lake and then walked between the pine trees into the forest. After they had walked through the forest, they walked down the path that led to the beach. When they reached the beach, they ran towards the water. They dived off the rocks into the rock pool.

Pronouns

Introduction

Third and fourth graders should understand that we use **pronouns** to take the place of nouns. By using pronouns we can talk about people or things without naming them. This helps to keep our language from becoming disjointed because of too much repetition.

Without pronouns we would have to write the following:

Bill said that Bill could not come because Bill's father had not bought Bill a new pair of sneakers.

Children can quickly see the need for pronouns when they read this.

There are many types of pronouns. Those appropriate for third and fourth grade students are the following:

(a) **Personal pronouns**—Here are the personal pronouns that students should be familiar with and be able to use without difficulty.

	Nominative		Objective	
	Singular	**Plural**	**Singular**	**Plural**
First person	I	we	me	us
Second person	you	you	you	you
Third person	he, she, it	they	him, her, it	them

Remember the following:

- If a pronoun is the **subject** or part of the subject of a sentence, it is in the **nominative case**.
  Example: *She* is coming to my house.

- If a pronoun is the **object** or **indirect object** in a sentence, it is in the **objective case**.
  Example: I gave *her* the book.

Pronouns (cont.)

- **First person** pronouns are used if we are talking about ourselves.
  Examples: *I* am nine years old.
  We are learning about sharks.

- **Second person** pronouns are used if we are talking to someone.
  Example: Are *you* going to be long?

- **Third person** pronouns are used if we are talking about someone or something else.
  Examples: *She* was late for school.
  They arrived by bus.
  It was on the table.

(b) **Possessive pronouns**—Students should also be familiar with the following possessive pronouns.

	Singular	**Plural**
First person	mine	ours
Second person	yours	yours
Third person	his, hers, its	theirs

Remember, some words look like pronouns but are really possessive adjectives. Look at the following sentences.

That book is *his*.   *His* is a possessive pronoun showing ownership.

His book is on the table.   *His* is a possessive adjective describing *book*.

For more information about possessive adjectives, see the section on adjectives.

(c) **Relative pronouns**—These not only take the place of nouns but also help join sentences. The main relative pronouns are the following:
who   *whom*   *which*   *that*

Who and whom are used to refer to people. *Who* is nominative case and is used when referring to the subject of the verb. *Whom* is objective case and is used when referring to the object of the verb.
    Examples: The girl *who* wore the blue hat is my sister.
             The friend with *whom* I went to the park lost his wallet.

Which and **that** are used to refer to animals, places, and things.

Pronouns (cont.)

Problem pronouns

its/it's

Its is a pronoun that means belonging to it. *It's* is not a pronoun. It is a contraction of *it is*.

I/me

Sometimes it is difficult to decide when to use *I* or *me* in a sentence. If in doubt, divide the sentence into two short sentences.

Mike is going to the circus.   *I am going to the circus.*

So the correct usage is *Mike and I are going to the circus.*

Jack told Sally to get off the grass.   *Jack told me to get off the grass.*

So the correct usage is *Jack told Sally and me to get off the grass.*

Teaching Strategies

Replace the noun

Write sentences on the board and have children suggest words that could replace the nouns.

Mike said that Mike would arrive as soon as Mike's bicycle was fixed.

This bicycle belongs to me. This bicycle is _____.

Hands up

Read a story and have children raise their hands when they hear a pronoun. This can also include nursery rhymes.

Little Miss Muffet,

Sat on *her* tuffet,

Eating *her* curds and whey.

Choose the pronoun

Have children choose the correct pronoun to complete a sentence.

Tom said, "Give it back to _____." (me   I)

Did you know _____ goes to Chicago each week? (he   him)

Pronoun cloze

Write a passage on the chalkboard, leaving spaces for the pronouns. Write the missing pronouns on small pieces of cardboard and have children work in groups to stick them in the correct spaces.

Jane carried the glass to the kitchen. At the sink _____ dropped _____.

Pronouns

Pronouns are words that take the place of nouns.

1. **Rewrite the story, using pronouns to replace the underlined nouns.**

   One day Susan and <u>Susan's</u> father went to the zoo. <u>Susan and Susan's father</u> travelled to the zoo in a bus. <u>Susan's father</u> took <u>Susan</u> to the zoo because it was <u>Susan's</u> birthday and <u>Susan</u> had always wanted to see the tigers that <u>Susan</u> had read about in the newspaper. The tigers were brought to the United States in the hope that <u>the tigers</u> would breed.

   _____

   _____

   _____

   _____

   _____

   _____

   _____

   _____

2. **Color red those boxes that contain a pronoun.**

dog	me	silly	it	him	running
I	happy	he	ten	paper	them
pencil	us	down	they	her	your
we	old	she	penguin	it	sink
book	you	blue	them	cup	their

Pronouns

Pronouns are words that take the place of nouns.

1. **Circle the correct pronoun.**

    a. The birds flew away when I scared (**those them**).

    b. That belongs to Ian; please give it back to (**him he**).

    c. Are you going to come with (**I me**)?

    d. Did (**us you**) get the milk?

    e. Mary can't come because (**her she**) is ill.

    f. Do you think (**them they**) will help us?

2. **Replace the underlined words with a pronoun. Rewrite the sentence.**

    a. The teacher said <u>the teacher</u> had a sore throat.

    b. The boy told his friend to get <u>the boy</u> an ice-cream cone.

    _____

    c. Sally's mother asked <u>Sally</u> to clean up the bathroom.

    _____

    d. Michael and I stopped when <u>Michael and I</u> became tired.

    _____

Pronouns

Pronouns are words that take the place of nouns.

1. Add a pronoun in each space.

   a. These books belong to me. These books are _____ .

   b. Does the piano belong to her? Is the piano _____?

   c. These cups belong to us. These cups are _____ .

   d. The new horse belongs to them. The new horse is _____.

   e. You must take responsibility. The responsibility is _____ .

2. Circle the correct pronoun.

   a. This is the house (**that whose**) Jack built.

   b. I saw the boy (**who which**) saved the drowning lady.

   c. Do you know (**whose who**) car that is?

   d. Is this the hen (**which who**) lays the large eggs?

   e. Do you know the girl (**who whose**) won the gold medal?

   f. Did you help the man (**who whose**) leg was broken in the accident?

Pronouns

Sometimes it is difficult to decide when to use *I* or *me* in a sentence. If in doubt, divide the sentence into two short sentences.

- *Mike is going to the circus. I am going to the circus.*
  So the correct usage is *Mike and I are going to the circus.*

- *Jack told Sally to get off the grass. Jack told me to get off the grass.*
  So the correct usage is *Jack told Sally and me to get off the grass.*

Circle the correct pronoun.

a. Bill and (**I me**) are going to the party.

b. Aunt Tanya sent presents to Katy and (**I me**).

c. Between you and (**I me**), I think the teacher is right.

d. There was trouble coming for Kyle and (**I me**).

e. I was sure that Leith and (**I me**) were in trouble.

f. Ian and (**I me**) received letters from Uncle Colin.

g. Zach and (**I me**) are going to the movies.

h. Susan asked Shane and (**I me**) to visit.

i. Mom, Dad, and (**I me**) are going shopping for a new car.

j. Would you like to come to the pool with Matt and (**I me**)?

Pronouns

Name _____   Grammar BLM **53**

Pronouns are words that take the place of nouns.

1. Circle all the pronouns.

One day, when I was out walking with some friends, I saw Billy and Ned crossing the road outside their house. They said they were going to the park. We said we would go with them, so Billy ran back inside to get her football. She said we had to be careful with it because it was a present from her uncle who was a famous football player.

2. Add a pronoun in each space.

a. Susan left _____ in the classroom.

b. Ian said _____ could run faster.

c. The cat was licking _____ fur.

d. There is the dog _____ bit the mail carrier.

e. We did not know _____ had stolen the money.

f. Katy told me that _____ was leaving right away.

g. Scott and Maggie lost_____ keys.

Conjunctions

Introduction

Conjunctions can join compound subjects and compound predicates as well as serve to create compound sentences.

> Examples: *compound subject—Jerrie and Mac went on a trip.*
> *compound predicate—They would sail and fly.*
> *compound sentence—Jerrie chose Russia, and Mac chose India.*

Point out to students that whenever sentences are joined by the conjunctions *and, but,* and *or,* a comma usually goes before the conjunction as in the compound sentence above.

- *coordinating conjunctions (to join groups of words, including compound subjects, predicates, and sentences): and, but, or*
- *subordinating conjunctions (to join main and subordinate clauses for complex sentences): when, while, since, though, until, although, unless, whether, because*
- *relative pronouns (to join main and subordinate clauses for complex sentences): who, whom, which, that*

Teaching Strategies

Glue for words

Tear a piece of paper in two and show children how it can be joined with glue or sticky tape. Now write two sentences on the board. Show children how these can be joined also, but this time instead of glue or sticky tape we use a comma and a conjunction.

I washed the dishes. Sally dried them.

I washed the dishes, and Sally dried them.

You must hurry. You will miss the train.

You must hurry, or you will miss the train.

Provide children with numerous simple and informal exercises, having them suggest words suitable to join the sentences.

After the join

Have children orally finish sentences you have written on the chalkboard.

We laughed when . . .

I have not seen him since . . .

I was scared because . . .

I will not help you unless . . .

Conjunctions 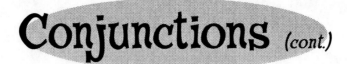 *(cont.)*

Use the conjunction
Provide children with exercises in which they use a given conjunction to join pairs of sentences.

Use a comma and *but*.

Mike is tall. Tom is short.   *Mike is tall, but Tom is short.*

A fire is hot. Ice is cold.   *A fire is hot, but ice is cold.*

Choose the conjunction
Provide a list of conjunctions on the chalkboard and have children finish sentences by using each one.

because   and   before

I cleaned my teeth _____ I went to bed.

We did not go _____ it was raining.

Tom grabbed the apple, _____ he ate it.

Conjunction search
Conduct a conjunction search from a common text, such as a photocopy of a story or poem already read. Have children read the text and circle any conjunctions they find.

Which conjunction?
Have children orally suggest suitable conjunctions for sentences which you read out loud.

I cannot come. My leg is sore. (if, because …)

In the beginning
Remind students that a conjunction need not necessarily come in the middle to join two sentences. Provide exercises encouraging children to begin the sentence with the conjunction.

He did not come. He is ill.

He did not come because he is ill.

Because he is ill, he did not come.

Conjunctions

Conjunctions are joining words. They are used to join words and whole sentences.

1. **Choose a word from the box to complete each sentence.**

> because   when   until   unless   and   if

   a. We must wait here _____ our parents arrive.
   b. The baby began to cry _____ the little boy pinched him.
   c. The thief stole the money _____ he wanted to buy a motorbike.
   d. The fish will not bite _____ you keep making all that noise.
   e. I dug up the soil, _____ Sally raked it over.
   f. You will not get on the team _____ you practice much harder.

2. **Make up as many sentences as you can by combining the groups of words in the boxes. If you need more space, write your sentences on the back of the sheet.**

Sally cried	because	her parents said it
Sally didn't come	although	would be alright.
Mike laughed	when	he missed the bus.
Tom yelled	until	she was not feeling well.
		the bus broke down.

_____

_____

_____

_____

_____

Conjunctions

Name _____ Grammar BLM 55

Conjunctions are joining words. They are used to join words and whole sentences.

On the first line, join the sentences by using a conjunction in the middle. On the second line, join the sentences by using a conjunction at the beginning.

a. We had a bath. We arrived home.

_____

_____

b. We ate a sandwich. It was lunchtime.

_____

_____

c. She did not come. She was grounded by her parents.

_____

_____

d. We still felt cold. We lit a fire.

_____

_____

e. Freya washed her hands. She ate her lunch.

_____

_____

f. The train was late. We still arrived on time.

_____

_____

g. Susan locked the doors. She left the house.

_____

_____

Conjunctions

Conjunctions are joining words. They are used to join words and whole sentences.

1. Use the words in the box to complete the sentences.

when	before	and	because

a. Mike did not come _____ he was feeling ill.

b. Susan boiled the eggs, _____ Jane cut the bread.

c. We must leave here _____ it begins to rain.

d. The birds flew away _____ they heard the sound of the guns.

2. Join each pair of sentences, using the word in the parentheses.

a. John could not lift the box. It was too heavy. (**because**)

_____

b. We will have brush fires. It is a hot summer. (**if**)

_____

c. I have not heard from him. I told him to go home. (**since**)

_____

d. We won the match. Our best players were unable to play. (**although**)

_____

Conjunctions

Conjunctions are joining words. They are used to join words and whole sentences.

1. Use a different conjunction to join the sentence in the box to each of the sentences below.

> ### Sally rode her bicycle.

a. Her father had told her to leave it at home.

_____

_____

b. She wanted to get there quickly.

_____

_____

c. Her mother said she couldn't take her in the car.

_____

_____

d. John ran along beside her.

_____

_____

e. She was so tired she couldn't ride any longer.

_____

_____

2. Finish the sentences in your own words.

Our team won the match . . .

   a. because _____

   b. although _____

   c. when _____

   d. so _____

   e. and _____

Conjunctions

Conjunctions are joining words. They are used to join words and whole sentences.

1. Add a conjunction to complete each sentence.

a. I missed the bus _____ I got up late.

b. The sun is shining _____ it is starting to snow.

c. Katy cleaned her teeth _____ went to bed.

d. _____ he broke his toy, the little boy began to cry.

e. We had a swim _____ we went to the beach.

f. _____ you do not hurry, you will be late.

2. Add a conjunction in each space.

Last week Sam _____ John did not go to the soccer match _____ they were not feeling well. They had not been feeling well _____ they ate some hamburgers they had bought down the street. Their parents told them they had to stay at home _____ they were better. The boys agreed with their parents _____ they both wished they could have seen the match.

Sentences

Introduction

A **sentence** is a group of words that makes sense and contains a subject and a verb. Take the example *into the box.* This is not a sentence as it does not have a subject and a verb and does not make sense by itself. A sentence begins with a capital letter and ends with a period, question mark, or exclamation mark.

There are four types of sentences.

(a) **Statements** simply state something or give information about something.

Examples: *It is hot.   The time is eight o'clock.   Koalas are marsupials.*

(b) **Questions** ask something.

Examples: *What is the weather like? What time is it?   What is a koala?*

(c) **Commands or requests** direct someone to do something. They can also give advice or warnings.

Examples: *Get out your books.   Sit up.   Look out for sharp stones.*

(d) **Exclamations** express the strong feeling of the speaker or writer about something.

Examples: *Ouch!   I did it!   What a fantastic day!*

Sentences can take several forms.

(a) **Simple sentences** consist of one clause. They can be divided into two parts: the subject tells who or what did something, and the **predicate** contains the verb and tells us what the subject did or is doing.

Examples: *Horses (subject) run (predicate).*

Billy (subject) climbed the tree (predicate).

Although the terms subject and predicate need not be mentioned at this level, it is important that students do come to see that a sentence tells us who or what did something and what they did.

(b) **Complex sentences** have more than one verb and thus have more than one clause. A complex sentence has at least one main clause and one or more subordinate clauses.

Example: *When it was hot we went for a swim because we wanted to get cool.*

(c) **Compound sentences** consist of two or more main clauses (independent clauses) joined by a comma and a conjunction.

Example: *I washed the dishes, and Billy dried them.*

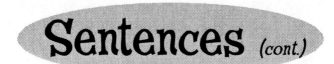

Speech can be reported directly or indirectly.

(a) **Direct speech** is the exact words spoken by a person. It is enclosed in quotation marks.

Examples: *"I am writing a story," said Meg.*
Meg said, "I am writing a story."
"I am," said Meg, "writing a story."

Notice that the commas and the periods appear inside the quotation marks.

(b) **Indirect speech** reports a person's speech but does not necessarily quote the exact words used.

Examples: *Meg said she is writing a story.*
Meg told us she was writing a story.

Teaching Strategies

Complete the sentence

Have children add words to complete a sentence. Informal exercises such as this demonstrate to children that a sentence must express a complete thought.
Bill has a new
I a rabbit

Answer the question

Ask children questions and have them answer in complete sentences. Children could also be organized in pairs and take turns to ask and answer questions. The game could be made more fun by allowing children to make up silly questions.
What is your name?
My name is Miles Joseph Smith.

Jumbled sentences

Write a series of jumbled sentences on the chalkboard. Challenge children to orally unjumble them. As children become more confident, try giving longer sentences.
lives dog a kennel in a

Interview

Choose volunteers to imagine that they have just returned from the moon. Have the rest of the class imagine that they are reporters and ask suitable questions which the moon travellers must answer in complete sentences.
Is the surface of the moon dry?
How long did it take you to get to the moon?

Select other volunteers to take on other roles for the class to question, for example, biologist, tennis player, firefighter.

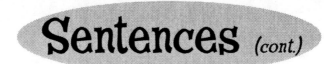
Sentences (cont.)

Complete the sentence
Have children complete sentences that you have begun or begin sentences that you have provided only the endings for. Activities such as this help children understand that sentences have a part that tells who or what did something and a part that tells what they did.

A spider . . .
A dog . . .
. . . swam across the creek.
. . . bit the boy on the leg.

Match up
Have children match the beginnings of sentences to the best endings.

The dog   get wool from sheep.
We   climbed the tree.
The monkey   barked at the stranger.

Headline hunt
Have children search through newspapers and cut out the headline words. Have them create sentences of their own using the words and then paste their sentences onto a sheet of paper.

What am I?
Read a description of an object and ask children to guess what it is. Point out the statements and question in the description, and ask children to answer with a complete sentence. Challenge children to make up their own "What am I?" statements and questions.

I am small. I have wings. I am an insect. I make honey.
What am I?
I am a bee.

Make the opposite
Write a sentence on the chalkboard. Have children rearrange the words to make the sentence mean the opposite.

The bull chased the boy.   The boy chased the bull.

Addo
Call out one word. Children must then add one word at a time to build up a long, sensible sentence. This can be played as a circle game.

Bill
Bill ran
Bill ran across
Bill ran across the . . . and so on.

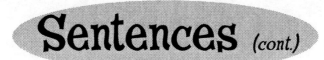

Sentences (cont.)

Subject/predicate match

On separate pieces of cards, write suitable subjects and predicates. Shuffle them and have children make sentences. Children can also make sets of cards for other groups to match.

The dog   are in the garden.

The girls   is climbing the tree.

The boy   is chewing its bone.

Sentence search

Have children search through a text to find the following:

the longest sentence

the shortest sentence

a question

an exclamation

a command

a statement

direct speech

indirect speech

Make a sentence

Have children make up their own sentences from given words.

farmer   sheep   meadow

The farmer drove the sheep into the meadow.

Sentence formulas

First, have children create sentences based on formulas and then let them make up sentence formulas for their classmates to "solve."

article + noun + verb   *The snake crawled.*

article + adjective + noun + verb   *The black snake crawled.*

article + adjective + noun + verb + adverb   *The black snake crawled away.*

Sentences

A sentence must make sense and must contain a subject and a verb.

1. **Rearrange the words to make a sentence.**

    a. the cat the jumped fence

    _____

    b. time the us tells clock a

    _____

    c. has a bicycle wheels two

    _____

    d. a legs donkey four has

    _____

    e. books read to Freya likes

    _____

2. **Underline the sentence in each pair and add the correct end punctuation.**

    a. The cat a mouse
       The cat has caught a mouse

    b. The teacher told us a story
       The teacher story

    c. Ned purse in the street
       Ned found a purse in the street

    d. The small girl ran into the house
       The small girl into the house

Sentences

A sentence must make sense and must contain a subject and a verb.

1. Circle the verb in each of these sentences.

a. I like dogs and cats.

b. Will you leave now?

c. Take that puppy out of here.

d. Mike has five hats in his wardrobe.

e. Tom's mother bought a new car.

f. Sally had her birthday party on Friday.

2. Complete each sentence by adding a suitable verb.

a. The dog _____ a rabbit.

b. Rebecca and Lucy _____ dresses of the same color.

c. The kangaroo _____ over the fence.

d. James _____ his new shoes to school.

e. Did you _____ the washing this morning?

f. My friend _____ on Wattle Street.

g. Eddie Mae _____ a long-distance call.

Sentences

Name _____   Grammar BLM

A sentence must make sense and must contain a subject and a verb.

Add a word to complete each sentence. Write the sentence on the line.

a. Last night it heavily.

_____

b. Have you ever to the lake?

_____

c. At the beach we every day.

_____

d. Why did you that small log?

_____

e. My dog can loudly.

_____

f. Ben has already this book.

_____

g. My best friend a motorbike.

_____

h. I the flowers in a vase.

_____

i. The truck down the street.

_____

j. We all the way to the park.

_____

Sentences

A sentence has a part that tells who or what did something (subject) and a part that tells what they did (predicate).

1. These sentences have been muddled. Rewrite each one with the correct subject and predicate.

Our teacher crowed loudly at six o'clock.
The kitten was riding his new bicycle.
A key is yellow when it is ripe.
A banana is used to open and lock doors.
The rooster read us a book about dinosaurs.
Mike was spinning around and trying to catch his tail.

a. _____

b. _____

c. _____

d. _____

e. _____

f. _____

2. Add a predicate to each subject.

a. The lion _____ .

b. The police officer _____ .

c. The teacher _____ .

d. The apple _____ .

Sentences

A sentence has a part that tells who or what did something (subject) and a part that tells what they did (predicate).

1. Draw lines to match each subject to its correct predicate.

   a. A pencil   makes us thirsty.

   b. A car   is a beautiful flower.

   c. Hot weather   is used to write with.

   d. A dentist   has roots and branches.

   e. A lion   looks at our teeth.

   f. A tree   has four wheels.

   g. A giant   is a type of large cat.

   h. A rose   is very large.

2. Add a subject to each predicate.

   a. _____ fell into the water.

   b. _____ have a new car.

   c. _____ feed my puppy every day.

   d. _____ won the game on the weekend.

Sentences

A sentence has a part that tells who or what did something (subject) and a part that tells what they did (predicate).

Use the words to make a sentence. You may add other words of your own. Don't forget to start with a capital letter and end with a period.

a. girl combed hair

_____

_____

b. dog found bone

_____

_____

c. boy fell river

_____

_____

d. hen laid egg

_____

_____

e. car crashed high wall

_____

_____

f. cat caught gray mouse

_____

_____

g. apple red ripe

_____

_____

h. we football Saturday morning

_____

_____

Sentences

A simple sentence is made up of one clause. It contains a subject and a predicate and makes sense on its own. The subject will contain a noun or pronoun, and the predicate will contain a verb. (*I washed the dishes.* I = subject, washed the dishes = predicate)

A compound sentence is made up of two or more main clauses joined by a comma and a coordinating conjunction. (*I washed the dishes, and Bill dried them.*)

A complex sentence is made up of a main clause and a subordinate or dependent clause. The clauses are joined by a subordinating conjunction or a relative pronoun. (*I washed the dishes while Bill dried them.*)

After each sentence write whether it is simple, compound, or complex.

a. The old man hobbled down the street.

_____

b. I ate an orange, and I ate an apple.

_____

c. We will go inside if it begins to rain.

_____

d. The police officer caught the thief who stole the jewels.

_____

e. I have read ten books this year.

_____

f. The hamburgers are delicious, and the pizza is too.

_____

g. We went to the zoo and saw the lions.

_____

h. I want to see that movie.

_____

Sentences

Name _____   Grammar BLM **66**

A simple sentence is made up of one clause. It contains a subject and a predicate and makes sense on its own. The subject will contain a noun or pronoun, and the predicate will contain a verb. (*I washed the dishes.* I = subject, washed the dishes = predicate)

A compound sentence is made up of two or more main clauses joined by a comma and a coordinating conjunction. (*I washed the dishes, and Bill dried them.*)

A complex sentence is made up of a main clause and a subordinate or dependent clause. The clauses are joined by a subordinating conjunction or a relative pronoun. (*I washed the dishes while Bill dried them.*)

1. **Complete these simple sentences by adding predicates.**

    a. The large dog _____.

    b. The bus driver _____.

2. **Complete these compound sentences by adding predicates.**

    a. The girls _____ , and the boys _____ .

    b. I _____ , and I _____ .

3. **Complete these complex sentences by adding subordinate conjunctions.**

    a. The picnic was lots of fun_____the rain began.

    b. The house_____ is near the station is very old.

4. **Make up a simple, compound, and complex sentence of your own.**

    a. Simple: _____

    b. Compound: _____

    c. Complex:_____

Sentences

Direct speech is the exact words spoken by a person. The words are usually enclosed in quotation marks.
"I am writing a story," said Meg.

Add the quotation marks where they are needed in these sentences.

a. I love cats, said Tom.

b. We are playing football today, yelled Mike.

c. Be careful. The teacher might catch you, whispered Joe.

d. What time will Sam arrive? asked Tom.

e. What a good idea! said the teacher.

f. Go! shouted the starter.

g. Fred yelled, Look out for the wild dog!

h. The girl in the red dress said, I will help you lift that.

i. My best friend Tom said, Can you stay at my house for the weekend?

j. My mother said, I've told you before that you are not going to the party.

k. The man at the shop said, It costs five dollars.

l. I know it's hot, said the teacher, but please try to concentrate.

Sentences

Indirect speech reports a person's speech but does not necessarily quote the exact words used. The words are not enclosed in quotation marks.
Paul said that he was coming.

Change the direct speech into indirect speech. Remember, you don't need to use the exact words that the person said.

a. "What time is it?" asked Nancy.

_____

b. "It is going to be a lovely day," remarked Sue.

_____

c. "Where are you going?" asked Paul.

_____

d. "I've read that book before," growled Tom.

_____

e. "I am going to win the race," boasted Jack.

_____

f. "Where will you get it from?" asked Sue.

_____

g. Mom said, "It's too hot to go shopping."

_____

h. "We want more hamburgers!" yelled the boys.

_____

Prepositional Phrases

Introduction

A **phrase** is a group of words without a subject and predicate. It functions as a single part of speech. A **prepositional phrase** consists of a preposition, a noun or pronoun that is its object, and any modifiers of the noun or pronoun.

Examples: Jon ate *at home*.   Jon ate *at the luxurious convalescent home*.

Prepositional phrases function as adjectives (to modify nouns and pronouns) and as adverbs (to modify verbs, adjectives, and adverbs).

(a) **Adjectival prepositional phrases** tell us more about or describe a noun or pronoun. They should be placed close to the noun or pronoun they modify.

Example: The <u>girl</u> *with long hair* is coming to the party.

(b) **Adverbial prepositional phrases** do the work of an adverb. They tell us more about verbs, adjectives, or adverbs. They tell how, when, or where an action occurs.

Examples: The boy kicked the ball *with a lot of skill*. (modifies verb "kicked")
Sally was rich *as a queen*. (modifies adjective "rich")
I run early *in the morning*. (modifies adverb "early")

Teaching Strategies

Add a preposition

Have children add a suitable preposition to begin a phrase.

The cow jumped _____ the moon.

The cow jumped over the moon.

Classroom phrases

Have children indicate the positions of certain objects in the classroom. Tell them that they must answer with a prepositional phrase.

Teacher: Tom, where is the television?

Tom: near the table

Circle the phrases

As children become more confident, have them search through sentences you have prepared, or through a photocopy of a familiar story, to find and circle the prepositional phrases.

Prepositional Phrases *(cont.)*

Suggest a phrase

Have children suggest prepositional phrases used as adjectives (to describe nouns or pronouns) or adverbs (to describe verbs, adjectives, and other adverbs) to complete sentences.

The bell rings *at nine o'clock.* (adverbial phrase modifies the verb <u>rings</u>)

I saw the girl *with red hair.* (adjectival phrase modifies the noun <u>girl</u>)

Complete the sentence

Provide plenty of short exercises for which children must select the more suitable phrase to complete a sentence.

The boy swam   in the pool.
*   on the roof.*

Make a sentence

Have children make up sentences that include given prepositional phrases.

before dawn   *We left before dawn.*
across the sky   *A jet roared across the sky.*

Opposite match

Have children match prepositional phrases with opposite meanings.

at dawn   *at sunset*
down the steps   *up the stairs*

Add a phrase

Have children add prepositional phrases of their own to make sentences more interesting.

We left the house.   *We left the house before noon.*
The girl fed the puppy. *The girl with red hair fed the puppy.*

Where should the phrase go?

Make up a number of sentences with the prepositional phrases incorrectly placed. Have children rewrite the sentences correctly.

The jet plane was piloted by a lady with four engines.
The jet plane with four engines was piloted by a lady.

How, when, or where?

Provide children with a number of sentences with adverbial prepositional phrases. Have them identify whether each tells how, when or where.

with a friendly smile (how)
in the box (where)
before nine o'clock (when)

Prepositional Phrases

A phrase is made up of several words but does not contain a subject-verb combination. The most common type of phrase is the prepositional phrase. It can function in a sentence as an adjective or an adverb.

1. For each prepositional phrase choose from the box a word that has a similar meaning.

> carefully   quickly   blind   hilly   bald   now

   a. without sight _____

   b. without hair _____

   c. at this moment _____

   d. at a great rate _____

   e. with great care _____

   f. with plenty of hills _____

2. Draw lines to link the prepositional phrases that have opposite meanings.

   a. inside the house   in a rude manner

   b. in the front   up the stairs

   c. in the morning   at night

   d. down the steps   at the back

   e. in a polite way   outside the house

   f. above the ground   beneath the soil

Prepositional Phrases

Name _____   Grammar BLM **70**

A phrase is made up of several words but does not contain a subject-verb combination. The most common type of phrase is the prepositional phrase. It can function in a sentence as an adjective or an adverb.

1. Choose the best prepositional phrase from the box to complete each sentence.

at the supermarket	before dinner	in the cage
into the pool	across the sky	with long, black hair

a. Sally put the bird back _____ .

b. The young girl _____ is my cousin.

c. I washed my hands _____ .

d. The large jet roared _____ .

e. We bought some milk _____ .

f. Max dived from the board _____ .

2. Underline the prepositional phrases in these sentences.

a. The rabbit dived into its burrow.

b. The monkey climbed up the tree.

c. We left camp before sunrise.

d. The car sped along the road.

e. There are many mushrooms under the tree.

f. The man with sunglasses is a film star.

Prepositional Phrases

Name _____   Grammar BLM

A phrase is a group of words without a subject or verb. Some prepositional phrases do the work of an adverb. They may tell *how*, *when*, or *where* an action happens.

1. Look at each underlined phrase. Write *how* if it tells how an action happens, *when* if it tells when an action happens, or *where* if it tells where an action happens.

   a. We will leave <u>before dark</u>.   _____

   b. We walked <u>through the long grass</u>.   _____

   c. The teacher spoke <u>with great care</u>.   _____

   d. I can jump <u>over that fence</u>.   _____

   e. I play baseball <u>during the week</u>.   _____

   f. Sally put the box <u>on the table</u>.   _____

2. Write a sentence of your own using each prepositional phrase as an adverb.

   a. just before sunset

   _____

   b. near the school

   _____

   c. on his front lawn

   _____

   d. until ten o'clock

   _____

Prepositional Phrases

Name _____   Grammar BLM **72**

A phrase is a group of words without a subject or a verb. Some prepostional phrases function as adverbs. They modify verbs, adjectives, and other adverbs. Others function as adjectives to modify nouns and pronouns.

1. **Choose the prepositional phrase that best completes each sentence.**

> in the cage   after the movie   during the afternoon
> with both hands   before school   at summer camp

   a. The boys did their work _____.

   b. I made lots of new friends _____.

   c. I lifted the heavy box _____.

   d. We played baseball _____.

   e. The parrots are now back _____.

   f. I went to bed _____.

2. **Add a prepositional phrase which tells how, when, or where an action happens to complete each sentence.**

   a. The bird laid three eggs _____.

   b. The snake crawled _____.

   c. The lady sneaked _____.

   d. We walked _____.

   e. You juggled _____.

Prepositional Phrases

Name _____   Grammar BLM **73**

Some prepositional phrases do the work of an adverb. They may tell how, when, or where an action happens.

We walked <u>into the classroom</u>.

Some prepositional phrases do the work of an adjective. They describe or add meaning to a noun or pronoun.

The girl <u>with red hair</u> is my sister.

Look at each underlined prepositional phrase. Write whether it is doing the work of an adverb or adjective.

a. He will be here <u>in a short time</u>.   _____

b. The girl <u>in a blue jumper</u> spoke to me.   _____

c. The man <u>with a gray beard</u> is my uncle.   _____

d. I put the books <u>on the table</u>.   _____

e. Jack walked <u>along the road</u>.   _____

f. Tom is the boy <u>with the black eye</u>.   _____

g. The girl <u>in the blue swimsuit</u> is a champion.   _____

h. I chose the book <u>behind the counter</u>.   _____

Clauses

Introduction

A **clause** is a group of words that contains a subject and a predicate. The subject of a clause may be expressed or understood. In the example *Stand up!* the subject *you* is understood.

There are two types of clauses.

(a) A **main clause** (independent clause) contains the main thought of the sentence and makes sense standing alone.

    Examples: *I spoke to the teacher* who is our football coach.
                 The dog that was barking *chased me across the lawn.*

(b) A **subordinate clause** (dependent clause) cannot make sense standing on its own. To make a sentence, a subordinate clause must be added to a main clause.

    Examples: I saw the dog *when I came home.*
                 They went to the shop *so they could buy ice cream.*

Subordinate clauses add information to a sentence and function in the same way as adjectives, adverbs, or nouns.

    Examples: The woman *who received the prize* is my mother. (adjective)
                 Our class stops working *when the bell rings.* (adverb)
                 I think *that we should always do the right thing.* (noun)

Sentences are analyzed by finding and naming the clauses.

(a) **Simple sentences** consist of one clause.

    Example: *Horses run.*

(b) **Complex sentences** have more than one subject-verb combination and thus have more than one clause. A complex sentence has at least one main clause and one or more subordinate clauses. A subordinate clause is introduced by a subordinating conjunction or a relative pronoun.

    Example: I was resting *while he was swimming laps.*

(c) **Compound sentences** consist of two or more main clauses (independent clauses)
joined by a conjunction.

    Example: *I washed the dishes, and Billy dried them.*

A clause may be linked with another clause by

- a subordinating conjunction.
    Examples: *when*   *where*   *while*   *if*   *because*

- a coordinating conjunction.
    Examples: *and*   *but*   *yet*   *or*   *for*

- a relative pronoun.
    Examples: *who*   *whom*   *whose*   *which*   *that*

Teaching Strategies

The main thing

Provide students with practice in finding the main clause in a sentence by having them search through a photocopy of a familiar story and circle the main clauses. Remind them that a main clause can stand alone and contains the main thought of the sentence. Point out that a simple sentence is, in fact, one main clause.

Main clause "beep"

Have children sit in a circle. Choose a child to say a word to start a clause. Each child in turn then adds a word to build a main clause. When the clause is complete, the next child says "Beep." The game can be extended to add a subordinate clause to the main clause.

Act the clause

Organize children in groups of four. Tell groups that the first child is to provide a subject, the second child is to provide a verb, the third child is to arrange the subject and a verb to make a clause, and the fourth child is to act out the clause. Ensure that all children get a turn in each role.

Clause match-up

Have children match main clauses to subordinate clauses. This is also an excellent reading activity.

These are the brave boys	*because he was feeling ill.*
Bill did not come	*where the bus stop was.*
The bus driver didn't know	*who rescued the drowning child.*

Clause call-out

Write a main clause on the chalkboard and challenge children to call out appropriate subordinate clauses.

We went to the park	*when we had eaten lunch.*
	where the banana tree grows.
	because we wanted to play.

Verb search

Write some clauses on the chalkboard. Have children search for and identify the verbs in each clause.

I saw the boy who broke the glass.

Clauses

A clause is a group of words that contains a verb and its subject. A main clause contains the main thought of the sentence and makes sense standing alone. A subordinate clause (dependent clause) does not make sense standing on its own. It adds information to the main clause.

1. Draw lines to match the main clauses to the correct subordinate clauses.

Main clause	Subordinate clause
a. We picked the mushrooms	because it began to rain.
b. The police spoke to the man	when leaves change color.
c. We left the picnic	after he washed his hands.
d. I asked the stranger	that grew under the trees.
e. Autumn is the season	who crashed his car.
f. Bill ate lunch	where he had come from.
g. Jill will attend	which was my stop.
h. The bus driver didn't know	if she has time.

2. Now choose two of the main clauses from number 1 and write new subordinate clauses for them. Write the sentences on the lines.

a.

_____

_____

b.

_____

_____

Clauses

A clause is a group of words that contains a verb and its subject. A main clause contains the main thought of the sentence and makes sense standing alone. A subordinate clause (dependent clause) does not make sense standing on its own. It adds information to the main clause.

1. Complete each sentence by adding a word from the box. Then circle the main clause in each sentence.

   who   because   that   where   whose   until

   a. We must wait here _____ the rain stops.

   b. Tom did not play _____ his foot was still sore.

   c. I met the boy _____ won the race.

   d. This is the dog _____ bit the postman.

   e. We walked _____ the brush was thick.

   f. I spoke to the teacher _____ son is in our grade.

2. Circle the main clauses. Underline the subordinate clauses.

   a. The children played where the ground was dry.

   b. Always look both ways before you cross a busy road.

   c. John cleaned his teeth after he had eaten his lunch.

   d. We are not going to school today because it is a holiday.

   e. We must leave after the first bell rings.

   f. I cannot help you because I am too busy.

Clauses

A clause is a group of words that contains a verb and its subject. The subject is the person or thing carrying out the action of the verb.

1. **Underline the verbs and circle the subjects in the following main clauses.**

   a. The boy hugged the dog.

   b. The black dog won the prize.

   c. The game lasted five hours.

   d. Was Michael in the house?

   e. The girls enjoyed the lesson.

   f. The mouse ran into the hole.

   g. The blue car won the race.

   h. The stables housed ten horses.

2. **Now write three main clauses of your own. Make sure they have a verb and a subject.**

   a. _____

   b. _____

   c. _____

Clauses

A clause is a group of words that contains a verb and its subject. The subject is the person or thing carrying out the action of the verb. Some clauses also contain an object. The object is the person or thing that something is being done to.

1. Underline the verb and circle the subject in the following main clauses. Now draw a box around the object.

   a. The boy bathed the dog.

   b. Luanna won the big prize.

   c. The kangaroo jumped the fence.

   d. The teacher praised the small boy.

   e. The savage dog bit the mailman.

   f. A tall boy won the race.

   g. Mr. Jones gave a speech.

   h. Dad mopped the floor.

2. Now write three main clauses of your own. Make sure they have a verb, a subject, and an object. (Do not use the verb "to be"—am, is, are, was, were, be, been—because it can not have an object.)

   a. _____

   b. _____

   c. _____

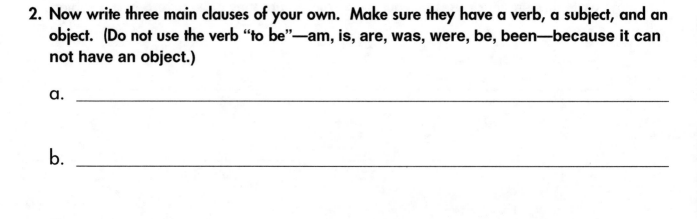

Punctuation

Introduction

An easy way to draw children's attention to the importance of punctuation is to make an analogy to the road signs we must obey.

> *A stop sign signals to a motorist that she must stop and not proceed until everything is clear. A period tells us we must stop a moment so that sentences do not run into each other and become difficult to understand. A yield sign tells a motorist to pause to ensure the traffic has passed. A comma tells us to pause to ensure the sentence makes sense. If all motorists obey the traffic signs, then cars, trucks, and bikes will travel along streets safely. If we all obey the punctuation signals, then we will be able to convey our thoughts and ideas clearly.*

The main elements of punctuation that third and fourth grade students should develop a working knowledge of are as follows.

A **capital letter** is used

(a) for the first letter of a sentence.

(b) for the first letter of a person's given name and family name.

(c) for the pronoun *I*.

(d) for the first letter of names of the days of the week, months of the year, and special times such as *Easter* and *Christmas*.

(e) for the first letter of names of towns, cities, countries, streets, schools, etc.

(f) sometimes to begin each line in poetry.

(g) for the first letter of the main words in the titles of books, poems, songs, and television programs.

A **period** is used

(a) at the end of a statement or command sentence.

Examples: *That dog is brown.* (statement)

              Sit down. (command)

(b) in abbreviations if the first letter and only part of the word is used.

Examples:
et cetera	*etc.*
captain	*capt.*
mister	*mr.*
doctor	*dr.*
road	*rd.*

Punctuation (cont.)

A **question mark** is used at the end of a sentence that is a direct question. It might be helpful to point out the question indicators *who, when, where, why, what,* and *how.*

Examples: *What is the time?* (direct question)

I asked her what the time was. (indirect question)

An **exclamation mark** is used at the end of a sentence that expresses a strong emotion. Point out to children that exclamation sentences are short.

Examples: *Wow!   Ouch!   Well done!*

Remind children to use only one exclamation mark. Using more than one does not create greater emphasis.

A **comma** is used

(a) to separate words in a list.

Examples: *Please go to the store and buy oranges, bread, milk, and butter.*
(separate nouns)

It was a big, black, hairy spider. (separate adjectives)

Please work quickly, neatly, and quietly. (separate adverbs)

(b) after the salutation in a friendly letter.

Example: *Dear Katy,*

(c) after the closing of a letter, before signing your name.

Example: *Yours faithfully,*

(d) to separate direct speech from the rest of the sentence.

Example: *"I hope he will be here soon," said Mike.*

Quotation marks are used to enclose direct speech (the words actually spoken by someone).

Examples: *Ali asked, "When are we going?"*

"Let's go now," said Ben.

An **apostrophe** is used

(a) in contractions to indicate where letters have been omitted.

Example: *I will   I'll*

(b) to indicate possession in nouns.

Examples: *a dog's kennel*

the three dogs' kennels

A **dash** is used

(a) to mark a change of thought or an abrupt turn in the sentence or to indicate faltering speech.

Example: *You can't do that—oh, you can.*

Punctuation (cont.)

(b) to indicate an unfinished or interrupted sentence.
Example: *But, Sir, I thought—*

(c) to enclose extra information. (Parentheses can also be used for this.)
Example: *Somewhere in Australia—I'm not sure of the exact spot—is a large deposit of gold.*

A **colon** is used to introduce more information. The information may be a list, words, phrases, clauses, or a quotation.

Example: *He bought lots of fruit: apples, pineapple, watermelon, bananas.*

A **semicolon** is used
(a) to join two related sentences.
Example: *I like jelly; my sister prefers ice cream.*

(b) to separate complex lists.
Example: *She brought a jacket with a hood; a coat with big pockets, a fur collar, and a matching scarf; and a large umbrella.*

Teaching Strategies

Don't pause for breath
Begin reading a story to the children but do not pause at any punctuation marks. The children will be confused and will all object to the speed of your reading. As soon as this happens, lead them into an informal discussion on the need for punctuation marks when we write.

"Beep" marks
Make cards that have large punctuation marks written on them. Read a simple story aloud to the children. Whenever you reach a punctuation mark, say "Beep!" The children must then hold up the missing mark.

What's the meaning?
From time to time challenge children by writing on the chalkboard a piece in which the meaning may be altered by incorrect punctuation.
Have you eaten Bill?   *Have you eaten, Bill?*
I have forty-two dollar coins.   *I have forty two-dollar coins.*

What a joke
Give children plenty of practice punctuating by writing unpunctuated jokes or riddles on the chalkboard. Have individual children add the punctuation in color.
what cat lives in the sea
an octopus

Punctuation

A capital letter is used for
- **the first letter of a sentence.**
- **the first letter in names—people, places, pets, days, months countries, states, towns, mountains, rivers.**
- **the pronoun _I_.**

1. **Rewrite the sentences, using correct punctuation.**

   a. the cow drank the water in the tank

   _____

   b. i saw nicky yesterday

   _____

   c. last monday ned and freya went to a movie

   _____

   d. next september julie is going to live in chicago

   _____

   e. sally is in grade three at preston elementary school

   _____

2. **Put a cross over the words that should not begin with a capital letter.**

   a. I know a tall Boy named John.
   b. Sally has a Dog called Rover and a Cat called Cuddles.
   c. There is a City called Chicago and a City called Kansas City.
   d. Mr. Smith has a Daughter named Ali.
   e. The largest School in our Town is Norwalk High School.

Punctuation

Name _____ Grammar BLM **79**

A capital letter is used for

- **the first letter of a sentence.**
- **the first letter in names—people, places, pets, days, months, countries, states, towns, mountains, rivers.**
- **the pronoun *I*.**
- **the main words in titles—books, songs, poems, etc.**

1. **Complete each sentence in your own words. Make sure you use capital letters and end punctuation where they are needed.**

    a. My two best friends are _____

    b. My birthday is in the month of _____

    c. My teacher's name is _____

    d. My favorite day of the week is _____

    e. A large city in Texas is _____

    f. Christmas is always in the month of _____

2. **Rewrite the sentences, using correct punctuation.**

    a. next saturday sally and peter are going to boston

    _____

    b. mike met mrs smith on spencer street

    _____

    c. the planet closest to pluto is neptune

    _____

    d. I read the book called <u>plants of north america</u>

    _____

    e. every easter and christmas we go on vacation to los angeles

    _____

©*Teacher Created Materials, Inc.*   119   *#3621 Grammar Practice—Grades 3–4*

Punctuation

Name _____

A statement sentence ends with a period. A question sentence ends with a question mark.

In each line there are two sentences. Punctuate them correctly.

a. my brother's name is david have you met him

_____

_____

b. the largest city in texas is houston have you been there

_____

_____

c. your dog rover is very large does he bark loudly

_____

_____

d. i read the book called <u>big home</u> have you read it

_____

_____

e. is that ian sitting over there why is he laughing

_____

_____

f. what is the tallest building in town is it the city library

_____

_____

g. what is this green vegetable is it spinach

_____

_____

h. why does a camel have a hump is it full of water

_____

_____

Punctuation

Commas are used to separate words in lists (or a series) and to show short pauses in writing.

1. Add commas where they are needed.

   a. The names of three fruits are pears apples and bananas.

   b. My best friends are Sally Michael and Julie.

   c. My favorite pets are dogs cats goldfish and white mice.

   d. The most popular sports in our school are baseball football golf and hockey.

   e. Four things you can write with are pencils crayons pens and chalk.

   f. The first four days of the week are Sunday Monday Tuesday and Wednesday.

2. Complete the sentences in your own words. Make sure you add commas where they are needed.

   a. The names of four children in my class are _____

   _____

   b. Four months of the year are _____

   _____

   c. The names of four creatures that live in water are _____

   _____

   d. The names of four birds are _____

   _____

   e. The names of four farm animals are _____

   _____

   f. The names of four vegetables are _____

   _____

Punctuation

A contraction is a word made by joining two words together and leaving out some of the letters. An apostrophe is used to show where the letters have been left out.

1. **Rewrite each sentence, replacing the underlined words with a contraction from the box.**

I'll	it's	don't	can't	isn't

a. Nicky <u>is not</u> coming to my house now. _____

_____

b. Jo <u>can not</u> help you today. _____

_____

c. Wise people <u>do not</u> run across busy roads. _____

_____

d. I think <u>it is</u> going to rain this morning. _____

_____

e. <u>I will</u> make sure he gets there on time. _____

_____

2. **Write the contractions of the underlined words.**

a. Max <u>does not</u> like playing football. _____

b. The crow <u>could not</u> find the nest. _____

c. Catherine <u>was not</u> at the movie last night. _____

d. If she <u>does not</u> hurry, <u>she will</u> be late. _____

Punctuation

An exclamation mark is used at the end of a sentence that expresses a strong emotion. Exclamation sentences are short.

1. **What might a person call out if the following happened? Write an exclamation from the box.**

> Ouch!   Look out!   How lovely!   Eek!   Yuck!

a. A ball is aimed at a group of small children. _____

b. You sit on a cactus. _____

c. You find a big, black spider in your desk. _____

d. You eat something that tastes terrible. _____

e. You see a vase of beautiful flowers. _____

2. **Add a period, question mark, or exclamation mark at the end of each sentence. Hint: There are three of each.**

a. Surprise

b. Seattle is a large city

c. Where is Paul going

d. Look out

e. What time is it

f. This book has lots of pages

g. I cut the lawn yesterday

h. When will you finish your lunch

i. That's amazing

Vocabulary

Introduction

Grammar is also concerned with the way an overall composition is structured to engage an audience and to deliver its message and with the way we choose particular words appropriate to that audience and message. It is important to generate an interest in words and to encourage children to be thoughtful about the words they use. If children develop an interest in language at an early age, they should continue throughout their school life and into adulthood appreciating the richness and diversity of our ever-growing language.

Concepts third and fourth graders should become familiar with follow.

Antonyms
An antonym is a word that has the opposite meaning to another word.

> Example: *absent/present*

Synonyms
A synonym is a word that has the same or a similar meaning to another word. Help children to understand that writers choose their words carefully and that one word may be more appropriate than another in a given situation.

> Example: *wed/marry*

Homonyms
There are two types.
(a) A **homophone** is a word that sounds the same as another word but has a different meaning and different spelling.
   Examples: *bear/bare*   *sun/son*

(b) A **homograph** is a word that is spelled the same as another word but has a different meaning.
   Examples: *I fished from the <u>bank</u> of the river.*
   I cashed the check at the <u>bank</u>.
   I don't think you should <u>bank</u> on it too much.

Anagrams
An anagram is a word that contains exactly the same letters as another word—but in a different arrangement.
   Examples: *palm/lamp*   *flow/wolf*

Partner words
These are words that are often paired together, especially in speech.
   Example: *salt and pepper*

Vocabulary (cont.)

Compound words
These are sometimes called "joined words." They are simply a large word made up of two or more smaller words. The combinations can be a noun and noun *(shell + fish = shellfish)* or an adjective and a noun *(black + bird = blackbird)*.

Similes
A simile is a figure of speech that compares one thing with another. It is a direct comparison introduced by the words *like* or *as*.

> Examples: *Her hair was like spun gold.*
> *The pavement was as hot as fire.*

Metaphors
A metaphor is an implied comparison. Rather than saying one thing is *like* another, a metaphor says that one thing *is* another.

> Example: *The clouds were full sacks ready to burst.*

Root words, prefixes, and suffixes
It is often helpful to see a word in terms of its various parts. These parts are called the root, the prefix, and the suffix.
The root word is the word from which other words are built.

> Example: *kind*

A prefix is a group of letters placed at the beginning of a word. It changes the meaning or use of the root word.

> Example: *un + kind = unkind*

A suffix is a group of letters added to the end of a word. (Sometimes spelling changes have to be made.) Suffixes also affect the meanings and uses of root words.

> Example: unkindly: *un*   *kind*   *ly*
> *prefix*   *root*   *suffix*

Teaching Strategies

Homophone hunt
Write a list of words on the chalkboard. Challenge children to think of the corresponding homophones. Children can also create cartoons to illustrate the homophones.

allowed/aloud	*ate/eight*	*eye/I*	*bare/bear*
bean/been	*blew/blue*	*board/bored*	*brake/break*
flea/flee	*hear/here*	*knit/nit*	*one/won*

Fish
On blank playing cards write pairs of synonyms, antonyms, or homophones. Encourage children to play "Go Fish" with them.

Vocabulary *(cont.)*

Sort the words

Supply children with numerous words written on small cardboard squares. Have children classify the words into categories.

animals: *cow*   *dog*   *cat*
birds: *crow*   *dove*   *sparrow*

Scattered letters

Write a selection of letters scattered on the chalkboard. Have children think of as many words as they can using the letters. Make the game more challenging by introducing a timer.

Word collection

Organize a word collection bulletin board in the classroom. Encourage children to find, collect, and then display words on the board. The board could have a number of different headings, such as Interesting Words, Words That Sound Funny, Words That Sound Like Noises, Words That Sound Important. Ask children to think of other headings they would like to use.

Tongue twisters

Challenge children to say a tongue twister quickly. Then have them make up their own tongue twisters for their friends to try.

Peter Piper picked a peck of pickled peppers.

Odd words

Have children search for words with interesting or unusual features. Here are some to start them off.

hijinks: *three dotted letters in a row*
strength: *eight letters but only one vowel*
subbookkeeper: *four sets of double letters*
facetious: *all the vowels in their correct order*
cauliflower: *contains all the vowels*
education: *contains all the vowels*

Daily letter race

Challenge children to write in two minutes all the words they can that begin with the first letter of that day of the week.

Compound Words

Compound words are words made by joining two or more words together.

1. **Add a word from the box to complete each compound word in the sentence.**

mother	brush	fish	corn	quake	pan

   a. At the beach we saw a jelly _____ .

   b. I cooked the eggs in the sauce _____ .

   c. I like to eat pop _____ for lunch.

   d. My grand _____ rides a motorbike.

   e. I cleaned my teeth with a tooth _____ .

   f. A terrible earth _____ struck the city.

2. **Join the words in box A to the words in box B to make compound words.**

A

| foot straw note break |
| hand egg photo life |

B

| cup boat fast book |
| berry ball graph cuffs |

_____   _____

_____   _____

_____   _____

_____   _____

Antonyms

An antonym is a word that has the opposite meaning to another word.

1. Write the word from the box that has the opposite meaning to the underlined word.

| thin | cruel | dead | glad | sharp | shallow |

   a. We swam in the <u>deep</u> end of the pool. _____

   b. I am <u>sorry</u> I was late. _____

   c. This pig is very <u>fat</u>. _____

   d. This knife is quite <u>blunt</u>. _____

   e. I am sure it is <u>alive</u>. _____

   f. Sam is very <u>kind</u> to animals. _____

2. Think of a word of your own that has the opposite meaning to the underlined word.

   a. We began to walk <u>inside</u> the room. _____

   b. The nuts on this wheel are quite <u>loose</u>. _____

   c. This animal is <u>dangerous</u> to touch. _____

   d. That line is very <u>straight</u>. _____

   e. This rock is <u>rough</u>. _____

   f. Kylie got all her sums <u>right</u>. _____

Synonyms

A synonym is a word that has the same or similar meaning to another word.

1. Write the word from the box that has a similar meaning to the underlined word.

| truck | reply | pester | discovered | sound | certain |

a. What was Kyle's <u>answer</u>?   _____

b. A large <u>van</u> carried the furniture away.   _____

c. I am <u>sure</u> she will arrive on time.   _____

d. I heard a strange <u>noise</u>.   _____

e. What did he say when he <u>found</u> the money?   _____

f. Dad told me not to <u>annoy</u> him any longer.   _____

2. Think of synonyms of your own for each of the following words. Compare your answers with those of a friend.

a. cure _____

b. fix _____

c. clever _____

d. strange _____

e. present _____

f. tiny _____

Homophones

A homophone is a word that sounds the same as another word but has a different meaning and different spelling.

1. **Use a word from the box to complete each sentence.**

> poor   wood   tail   hear   pour   would   tale   here

a. Our teacher told us a _____ about a dinosaur.

b. Did you _____ the roar of the lions at the zoo?

c. We cut some _____ to make a campfire.

d. I asked Leith to _____ the water in the bottle.

e. The dog spun around and tried to bite its own _____ .

f. I asked her to leave the books right _____ .

g. He was too _____ to buy even a hamburger for lunch.

h. He said he _____ come if he was allowed to.

2. **Circle the correct word in parentheses.**

a. It is rude to (**stair stare**) at people.

b. The old ship was (**towed toad**) out to sea and sunk.

c. Did you (**meet meat**) our new teacher?

d. I brushed the horse's (**main mane**).

e. This car is made of special (**steel steal**).

f. She was too (**week weak**) to leave the hospital.

Homographs

A homograph is a word that is spelled the same as another word but has a different meaning.

1. **Use a word from the box to complete each sentence. You will need to use each word twice.**

bark	rock	bank

   a. The dog began to _____ at the stranger.

   b. The _____ of the river is quite steep here.

   c. The silly boy threw a _____ at the window.

   d. I save my money in the _____.

   e. The huge waves began to _____ the boat.

   f. She made a canoe from the _____ of the tree.

2. **Write two sentences for each word. Make sure that each sentence gives the word a different meaning.**

   post

   a. _____

   b. _____

   well

   a. _____

   b. _____

   bat

   a. _____

   b. _____

Anagrams

An anagram is a word made by rearranging all the letters of another word.

1. **Rearrange all the letters of the word to make a new word to match the definition.**

   a. pea   large monkey   _____

   b. pale   to jump   _____

   c. side   stops living   _____

   d. tar   animal like a mouse   _____

   e. item   a clock tells it   _____

   f. pat   to hit lightly   _____

   g. lap   a friend   _____

2. **Rearrange the letters of the word in parentheses to make a new word to complete the sentence.**

   a. I ate a _____ with my hotdog. (**nub**)

   b. I am going to _____ this letter. (**spot**)

   c. I gave my brother a spinning _____. (**pot**)

   d. I cooked the food in the _____. (**nap**)

   e. I think my father is _____ not to let me go. (**mane**)

   f. I rode the _____ across the arena. (**shore**)

Root Words

A root word is a word from which other words are built.
A prefix is a group of letters placed at the beginning of a word.
A suffix is a group of letters added to the end of a word.

1. Write the root word.

a. indoors   _____

b. unwashed   _____

c. disagreement   _____

d. awaken   _____

e. unfinished   _____

f. enjoyable   _____

2. Rearrange the order of the prefix, root word, and suffix to make the word.

a. bolt un ed   (not locked)   _____

b. appear dis ed (to go out of sight)   _____

c. phone tele d   (dialed)   _____

d. ful truth un   (telling lies)   _____

e. ed un claim   (not claimed)   _____

f. ing re build   (building again)   _____

Similes

**A simile is a figure of speech that compares one thing to another.
It is a direct comparison introduced by the words *like* or *as*.**

1. Use a word from the box to complete each simile.

> grass   snow   owl   bone   ice   bee   mouse   bat

a. as green as _____

b. as white as _____

c. as dry as a _____

d. as wise as an _____

e. as blind as a _____

f. as busy as a _____

g. as cold as _____

h. as quiet as a _____

2. Rearrange the jumbled word to complete each simile.

a. as sharp as a (**ckta**) _____

b. as fat as a (**gip**) _____

c. as slow as a (**ailsn**) _____

d. as hot as a (**refi**) _____

e. as brave as a (**ilon**) _____

f. as heavy as (**adle**) _____

Answer Key

page 13
1.
   a. puppy
   b. coat
   c. flag
   d. pie
   e. apple
   f. atlas
   g. creek
   h. rain
2.
   a. bottle
   b. paper
   c. monkey
   d. boat
   e. mouse
   f. shop
   g. milk
   h. petal

page 14
1.
   a. canoe
   b. peach
   c. kitten
   d. snail
   e. lion
   f. kettle
   g. shirt
   h. piano
   i. swan
   j. ant
   k. gold
   l. golf
2.

c	a	r	h	a	t
b	b	a	l	e	f
u	o	r	o	a	o
s	x	m	g	r	x
i	c	e	k	e	y

page 15
1.
   a. deer
   b. snail
   c. feather
   d. ant
   e. bat
   f. ice
   g. sugar
   h. fire
2.
red boxes/parts of body
   ear
   nose
   eye
   teeth
   hand
   toe
   elbow
   hair
   ankle
   neck
blue boxes/parts of home
   window
   bedroom
   door
   curtain
   carpet
   cupboard
   roof
   shelf
   bathroom
   floor

page 16
1.
Things we eat
   honey
   jam
   ice cream
   butter
   bread
   pies
Things we can't eat
   tree
   wood
   sand
   cups
   cardboard
   ropes
2.
Things with four legs
   chair
   stool
   lion
   elephant
   table
   cow

Things with two legs
   magpie
   lady
   boy
   ladder
   sparrow
   penguin

page 17
1.
   a. countries
   b. days
   c. students
   d. months
   e. cities
   f. planets

2.
   Tuesday
   July
   Michael
   Disneyland
   California
   Joanna
   Rover
   Christmas

page 18
(Answers will vary.)

page 19
1.
   a. herd
   b. bunch
   c. swarm

Answer Key *(cont.)*

page 19 *(cont.)*
  d. forest
  e. flock
2.
  string
  box
  deck
  bundle
  album
  brood
3.
  a. birds
  b. insects
  c. fruit
  d. furniture

page 20
1.
Animals
  zebra
  horse
  giraffe
  lion
Birds
  swan
  dove
  emu
  eagle
Fruit
  banana
  apple
  pear
  peach
Furniture
  chair
  desk
  stool
  table
2.
  a. people
  b. flowers
  c. vegetables
  d. meat
  e. fruit
  f. countries

3.
  a. students
  b. players
  c. grapes
  d. cards
  e. people
  f. beads

page 21
1.
  a. watches
  b. dresses
  c. trees
  d. wishes
  e. brushes
  f. classes
2.
  a. men, leaves
  b. cats
  c. birds, trees
  d. horses
  e. donkeys
  f. buses, schools
3.
  a. children
  b. balls
  c. boats
  d. mice
  e. monkeys
  f. men

page 22
1.
  a. toys
  b. cities
  c. ladies
  d. puppies
  e. carts
  f. parties
2.
  a. fly
  b. donkey
  c. jelly
  d. cherry
  e. sky
  f. ray

3.
  a. wolves
  b. knives
  c. thieves
  d. shelves
  e. halves
  f. lives

page 23
1.
  a. the dog's ears
  b. the cat's claws
  c. the baby's rattle
  d. the teacher's car
  e. the bird's beak
2.
  a. sister's
  b. Katy's
  c. woman's
  d. father's
  e. man's
3. (Answers will vary)
  a. horse's
  b. cow's
  c. lady's
  d. car's

page 24
1.
  a. the dogs' ears
  b. the babies' toys
  c. the dogs' food
  d. the cars' engines
  e. the children's hats
2.
  a. children's
  b. horses'
  c. birds'
  d. clowns'
  e. men's
3. (Answers will vary.)
  a. cats'
  b. cows'
  c. women's
  d. students'

Answer Key *(cont.)*

page 25
1.
   a. doctor/dr.
   b. manager/mgr.
   c. colonel/col.
   d. detective/det.
   e. lieutenant/lt.
   f. captain/capt.
   g. sergeant/sgt.
   h. major/maj.
   i. prime minister/p.m.
   j. professor/prof.
2.
   a. Capt.
   b. Prof.
   c. Dr.
   d. Ms.
   e. Det.
   f. Mr.

page 26
1. *proper nouns*
   a. Richmond
   b. Simone
   c. John Jones
   d. Cuddles
   e. November
   f. Indiana
   g. Mary Jones
   h. Tuesday
   i. Springfield
2. *common nouns*
   brother
   home
   city
   train
   town
   grandparents
   farm
   lunch
   grandfather
   bales
   hay
   pickup
   dog
   cat

page 27
1.
   a. herd
   b. book
   c. deck
   d. class
   e. flock
   f. swarm
2.
   lions
   trees
   flies
   lions
   them
   their
   tails
   branches
   trees
   monkeys
   were
   lions
   their
   manes
3.
   a. jelly
   b. bus
   c. lady
   d. city
   e. leaf
   f. half

page 31
1. (Answers will vary.)
2.
On the soccer field
   dribble
   run
   kick
At school
   correct
   write
   read
In the garden
   dig
   water
   rake

page 32
1.
   a. washed
   b. pick
   c. ride
   d. hide
   e. stirs
   f. scratch
2.
   a. ate, tree
   b. rocked, cradle
   c. washed, soap
   d. rode, path

page 33
1.
   a. quacked
   b. yelled
   c. tell
   d. said
   e. talk
   f. screamed
2. (Answers will vary.)

page 34
1.
   a. think
   b. like
   c. felt
   d. believed
   e. understand
   f. embarrassed
2. (Answers will vary.)

page 35
   a. loves/thinking
   b. Race/action
   c. whispered/saying
   d. cheered/saying
   e. wish/thinking
   f. barks/saying
   g. believe/thinking
   h. told/saying
   i. galloped/action
   j. dreamed/thinking
   k. shared/action

Answer Key *(cont.)*

page 36

1.
   a. I was a skater.
   b. Freya and Katy played soccer.
   c. Mike wanted a pizza.
   d. Mr. Smith was a popular teacher.
   e. A black cat was good luck.
   f. I practiced the piano.

2.
   a. past
   b. future
   c. present
   d. present
   e. past
   f. future

page 37

1.
   a. rang
   b. rode
   c. saw
   d. ate
   e. drew
   f. was

2. (Answers will vary.)
   a. will ring
   b. will ride
   c. will see
   d. will eat
   e. will draw
   f. will be

page 38

circled verbs

sit	comes
eat	jump
bite	go
hurts	trip
feel	crash
go	stand
walk	bang
see	is
think	go
is	

past tense

sat	came
ate	jumped
bit	went
hurt	tripped
felt	crashed
went	stood
walked	banged
saw	was
thought	went
was	

page 39

1.
   Mrs. West
   dog
   Susan
   batter
   I
   grandfather

2. *subject/verb*
   Zach/sees
   swimmers/dived
   You/need
   we/hear
   she/lost
   (bike) riders/raced

page 40

1. *subject/* (Answers will vary.)
   (The) horse
   Jan
   Tom
   (The) monkey
   (Two) boys
   (The) cat

2.
   a. The monkey ate a banana.
   b. The captain kicked a goal.
   c. A snake bit the boy.
   d. Some girls played a ball game.
   e. The farmer milked the cow.
   f. Tom read a book.

page 41

1.
   a. run
   b. plays
   c. swims
   d. like
   e. sits
   f. write

2.
   is
   is
   are
   are
   is
   are
   are
   is

page 46

1.
   a. empty
   b. open
   c. fast
   d. soft
   e. raw
   f. strong

2.
   a. green
   b. black
   c. blue
   d. red
   e. white
   f. brown

page 47

1.
   a. sharp
   b. tiny
   c. long
   d. huge
   e. savage
   f. hard

2. (Answers will vary.)

Answer Key *(cont.)*

page 48

1.
fast runner
open door
hard rock
hot fire
deep water
interesting book
dark hair
ripe peach

2.
a. tall
b. old
c. clean
d. blue
e. neat
f. deep

page 49

1.
circled adjectives
best
black
large
brown
busy
rubber
strange
tall
oak
highest
broken
brown
strong
a. large, brown
b. best
c. black
d. busy
e. strange
f. broken

2. (Answers will vary.)

page 50

1., 2. (Answers will vary.)

page 51

1.
a. twelve
b. five
c. eight
d. two
e. four

2.
Thirty
Two
first
second
second
third
fourth
one hundred
forty
tenth

page 52

1.
a. These/those or Those/these
b. This/that or That/this
c. These/those or Those/these
d. These/those or Those/these

2.
a. her/its
b. My/Their/Her/Our/Your
c. my/their/her/our/your
d. My/Her/Your
e. (several possible combinations)

page 53

1.
a. stronger
b. hotter
c. redder
d. heavier
e. luckier
f. more delicious

2.
a. hottest
b. safest
c. most reliable
d. biggest

e. noisiest
f. bravest

page 54

1.
smoother, smoothest
thin, thinner
lucky, luckiest
wiser, wisest
delicate, most delicate
green, greener
best

2.
a. older
b. better
c. hottest
d. colder

page 57

1.
a. greedily
b. gently
c. silently
d. easily
e. slowly
f. noisily

2. (Answers will vary.)

page 58

1.
a. happily
b. loudly
c. quickly
d. easily
e. carefully
f. proudly

2.
a. strongly
b. sadly
c. loudly
d. softly
e. neatly
f. slowly

Answer Key *(cont.)*

page 59

1.
   a. near
   b. somewhere
   c. there/here
   d. out
   e. everywhere
   f. here/there

2. (Answers will vary.)

page 60

1.
   a. soon
   b. now
   c. yesterday
   d. today
   e. later
   f. often

2. (Answers will vary.)

page 61

1.
   a. where
   b. how
   c. where
   d. when
   e. when
   f. how

2.
   a. quickly
   b. soon
   c. here
   d. loudly
   e. there
   f. now

page 62

1.
   a. higher
   b. better
   c. easier
   d. best
   e. fastest
   f. more
   g. longer
   h. loudest

2.
   a. better, best
   b. fast, faster, fastest

page 64

1.
   miscellaneous
   education
   cauliflower
   facetious

2.
   a. seven
   b. orange
   c. horse
   d. carrot
   e. near
   f. camel

3. (Answers will vary.)

page 65

1.
   a. an
   b. A
   c. A
   d. an
   e. a
   f. a
   g. an
   h. a

2. (Answers will vary.)

3. (Answers will vary.)

page 66

1.
   a. an
   b. a/the
   c. the
   d. the/a
   e. an
   f. the/a
   g. An/The
   h. the

2.
   a
   the
   the
   a

   a
   a
   a
   the/an
   a/the
   an/the
   a/the
   the/a
   The
   the
   the/a

page 69

1.
   a. in
   b. during
   c. over
   d. through
   e. under
   f. up

2.
   a. at
   b. with
   c. off
   d. of
   e. for
   f. into

page 70

1. (Answers will vary.)

2. (Answers will vary.)

page 71

1.
   a. over
   b. outside
   c. after
   d. above
   e. off
   f. around

2. (Answers will vary.)

page 72

1. (Answers will vary.)

2.
   across
   between
   into

Answer Key (cont.)

page 72 (cont.)
through
down
to
towards
off
into

page 76

1.
her
They
He
her
her
she
she
they

2. *red boxes*

I	they
we	them
me	him
us	her
you	it
he	them
she	your
it	their

page 77

1.
a. them
b. him
c. me
d. you
e. she
f. they

2.
a. she/he
b. him
c. her
d. we

page 78

1.
a. mine
b. hers
c. ours

d. theirs
e. yours

2.
a. that
b. who
c. whose
d. which
e. who
f. whose

page 79

a.	I	f.	I
b.	me	g.	I
c.	me	h.	me
d.	me	i.	I
e.	I	j.	me

page 80

1.

I	her
I	She
their	we
They	it
they	it
We	her
we	who
them	

2. (Answers will vary.)

page 83

1.

a.	until	d.	if
b.	when	e.	and
c.	because	f.	unless

2. (Answers will vary.)

page 84

(Answers will vary.)

page 85

1. (Answers may vary.)
a. because
b. and
c. before
d. when

2.
a. John could not lift the box because it was too heavy.

b. We will have brush fires if it is a hot summer.
c. I have not heard from him since I told him to go home.
d. We won the match although our best players were unable to play.

page 86

1., 2. (Answers will vary.)

page 87

1., 2. (Answers will vary.)

page 92

1.
a. The cat jumped the fence.
b. A clock tells us the time.
c. A bicycle has two wheels.
d. A donkey has four legs.
e. Freya likes to read books.

2.
a. The cat has caught a mouse.
b. The teacher told us a story.
c. Ned found a purse in the street.
d. The small girl ran into the house.

page 93

1.
a. like
b. Will leave
c. Take
d. has
e. bought
f. had

2. (Answers will vary.)

page 94

(Answers will vary.)

page 95

1.
a. The rooster crowed loudly at six o'clock.
b. Mike was riding his new bicycle.
c. A banana is yellow when it is ripe.
d. A key is used to open and lock doors.

Answer Key *(cont.)*

page 95 *(cont.)*

  e. Our teacher read us a book about dinosaurs.

  f. The kitten was spinning around and trying to catch his tail.

2. (Answers will vary.)

page 96

1.

  a. A pencil is used to write with.

  b. A car has four wheels.

  c. Hot weather makes us thirsty.

  d. A dentist looks at our teeth.

  e. A lion is a type of large cat.

  f. A tree has roots and branches.

  g. A giant is very large.

  h. A rose is a beautiful flower.

2. (Answers will vary.)

page 97

(Answers will vary.)

page 98

  a. simple   e. simple

  b. compound   f. compound

  c. complex   g. simple

  d. complex   h. simple

page 99

1., 2., 3., 4. (Answers will vary.)

page 100

  a. "I love cats," said Tom.

  b. "We are playing football today," yelled Mike.

  c. "Be careful. The teacher might catch you," whispered Joe.

  d. "What time will Sam arrive?" asked Tom.

  e. "What a good idea!" said the teacher.

  f. "Go!" shouted the starter.

  g. Fred yelled, "Look out for the wild dog!"

  h. The girl in the red dress said, "I will help you lift that."

  i. My best friend Tom said, "Can you stay at my house for the weekend?"

  j. My mother said, "I've told you before that you are not going to the party."

  k. The man at the shop said, "It costs five dollars."

  l. "I know it's hot," said the teacher, "but please try to concentrate."

page 101

(Answers will vary.)

page 104

1.

  a. blind

  b. bald

  c. now

  d. quickly

  e. carefully

  f. hilly

2.

  a. inside the house/outside the house

  b. in the front/at the back

  c. in the morning/at night

  d. down the steps/up the stairs

  e. in a polite way/in a rude manner

  f. above the ground/beneath the soil

page 105

1.

  a. in the cage

  b. with long, black hair

  c. before dinner

  d. across the sky

  e. at the supermarket

  f. into the pool

2.

  a. into its burrow

  b. up the tree

  c. before sunrise

  d. along the road

  e. under the tree

  f. with sunglasses

page 106

1.

  a. when

  b. where

  c. how

  d. where

  e. when

  f. where

2. (Answers will vary.)

page 107

1.

  a. before school

  b. at summer camp

  c. with both hands

  d. during the afternoon

  e. in the cage

  f. after the movie

2. (Answers will vary.)

page 108

  a. adverb

  b. adjective

  c. adjective

  d. adverb

  e. adverb

  f. adjective

  g. adjective

  h. adjective

page 111

1.

  a. that grew under the trees.

  b. who crashed his car.

  c. because it began to rain.

  d. where he had come from.

  e. when leaves change color.

  f. after he washed his hands.

  g. if she has time.

  h. which was my stop.

2. (Answers will vary.)

page 112

1. *word/main clause*

  a. until, We must wait here

  b. because, Tom did not play

  c. who, I met the boy

Answer Key (cont.)

page 112 (cont.)
- d. that, This is the dog
- e. where, We walked
- f. whose, I spoke to the teacher

2. *main/subordinate*
- a. The children played/where the ground was dry
- b. Always look both ways/before you cross a busy road
- c. John cleaned his teeth/after he had eaten his lunch
- d. We are not going to school today/because it is a holiday
- e. We must leave/after the first bell rings
- f. I cannot help you/because I am too busy

page 113

1. *verb/subject*
- a. hugged/boy
- b. won/dog
- c. lasted/game
- d. Was/Michael
- e. enjoyed/girls
- f. ran/mouse
- g. won/car
- h. housed/stables

2. (Answers will vary.)

page 114

1. *verb/subject/object*
- a. bathed/boy/dog
- b. won/Luanna/prize
- c. jumped/kangaroo/fence
- d. praised/teacher/boy
- e. bit/dog/mailman
- f. won/boy/race
- g. gave/Mr. Jones/speech
- h. mopped/Dad/floor

2. (Answers will vary.)

page 118

1.
- a. The cow drank the water in the tank.
- b. I saw Nicky yesterday.

- c. Last Monday Ned and Freya went to a movie.
- d. Next September Julie is going to live in Chicago.
- e. Sally is in grade three at Preston Elementary School.

2.
- a. Boy
- b. Dog, Cat
- c. City, City
- d. Daughter
- e. School, Town

page 119

1. (Answers will vary.)

2.
- a. Next Saturday Sally and Peter are going to Boston.
- b. Mike met Mrs. Smith on Spencer Street.
- c. The planet closest to Pluto is Neptune.
- d. I read the book called *Plants of North America.*
- e. Every Easter and Christmas we go on vacation to Los Angeles.

page 120

1.
- a. My brother's name is David. Have you met him?
- b. The largest city in Texas is Houston. Have you been there?
- c. Your dog Rover is very large. Does he bark loudly?
- d. I read the book called *Big Home.* Have you read it?
- e. Is that Ian sitting over there? Why is he laughing?
- f. What is the tallest building in town? Is it the city library?
- g. What is this green vegetable? Is it spinach?
- h. Why does a camel have a hump? Is it full of water?

page 121

1.
- a. The names of three fruits are pears, apples, and bananas.
- b. My best friends are Sally, Michael, and Julie.
- c. My favorite pets are dogs, cats, goldfish, and white mice.
- d. The most popular sports in our school are baseball, football, golf, and hockey.
- e. Four things you can write with are pencils, crayons, pens, and chalk.
- f. The first four days of the week are Sunday, Monday, Tuesday, and Wednesday.

2. (Answers will vary.)

page 122

1.
- a. isn't
- b. can't
- c. don't
- d. it's
- e. I'll

2.
- a. doesn't
- b. couldn't
- c. wasn't
- d. doesn't, she'll

page 123

1.
- a. Look out!
- b. Ouch!
- c. Eek!
- d. Yuck!
- e. How lovely!

2.
- a. !
- b. .
- c. ?
- d. !
- e. ?
- f. .
- g. .
- h. ?
- i. !

Answer Key (cont.)

page 127
1.
   a. fish
   b. pan
   c. corn
   d. mother
   e. brush
   f. quake
2.
   football
   strawberry
   notebook
   breakfast
   handcuffs
   eggcup
   photograph
   lifeboat

page 128
1.
   a. shallow
   b. glad
   c. thin
   d. sharp
   e. dead
   f. cruel
2. (Answers will vary.)

page 129
1.
   a. reply
   b. truck
   c. certain
   d. sound
   e. discovered
   f. pester
2. (Answers will vary.)

page 130
1.
   a. tale
   b. hear
   c. wood
   d. pour
   e. tail
   f. here
   g. poor

   h. would
2.
   a. stare
   b. towed
   c. meet
   d. mane
   e. steel
   f. weak

page 131
1.
   a. bark
   b. bank
   c. rock
   d. bank
   e. rock
   f. bark
2. (Answers will vary.)

page 132
1.
   a. ape
   b. leap
   c. dies
   d. rat
   e. time
   f. tap
   g. pal
2.
   a. bun
   b. post/stop
   c. top
   d. pan
   e. mean
   f. horse

page 133
1.
   a. door
   b. wash
   c. agree
   d. wake
   e. finish
   f. joy
2.
   a. unbolted

   b. disappeared
   c. telephoned
   d. untruthful
   e. unclaimed
   f. rebuilding

page 134
1.
   a. grass
   b. snow
   c. bone
   d. owl
   e. bat
   f. bee
   g. ice
   h. mouse
2.
   a. tack
   b. pig
   c. snail
   d. fire
   e. lion
   f. lead